73652

To

WILLIAM MARSHALL COULTHARD

THE ORGAN

ITS TONAL STRUCTURE
AND REGISTRATION

by

CECIL CLUTTON

and

Lieut.-Colonel GEORGE DIXON, T.D., M.A.
(late The Border Regiment)

073652

1950

GRENVILLE PUBLISHING COMPANY LTD.
15-17, CITY ROAD, LONDON, E.C.1.

FOREWORD

In writing this book we have been constantly encouraged by many friends. Foremost among these was the late Sir Walter Alcock, M.V.O., Mus. Doc., who, in the last few months of his long life, read our manuscript in its preparatory stages. He wrote to us as follows :—

" This book has long been needed. The study of organ-playing must include a knowledge of the instrument, while a thorough understanding of its historical and technical aspects is an essential part of any organist's equipment if he is to be a true exponent of its beauties. A good deal of space is devoted to the tonal structure of the organ, but this is only done as a necessary approach to the subject of Registration, *which is the real object of the book. It is indeed high time that this important aspect of organ-playing received more widespread and systematic study."*

We are sincerely grateful to Dr. G. T. Thalben-Ball, who has recently written the following words, which, with those of Sir Walter Alcock, serve as the finest possible foreword to our book :—

" I have read the book from cover to cover with great interest and feel sure it will be of inestimable value to all students of the organ, whether amateur or professional. It is full of ideas which, even if one is not always in agreement, give lively cause for thought and study. It is a book which will satisfy a real need, and I am indeed grateful to the authors

for putting so much very useful information together in a clear and concise way."

Much help has been received from Dr. W. L. Sumner and Mr. Geraint Jones. We wish to thank " Musical Opinion Ltd" for so kindly permitting us to use much of the matter from articles in Volume I and XXIV of the " Organ " in Chapters III and IV of this book, respectively. We also thank Messrs. Henry Willis and Sons Ltd. for allowing us to quote, in Chapter II, from Mr. Guy Weitz's article on Registration in Volume II of " The Rotunda." Mr. John Compton has helped us greatly in dealing with the " Extension " organ. We also owe much to Mr. Austin Niland for the care and trouble he has taken in reading the proofs.

Finally, we are deeply indebted to Mr. W. M. Coulthard, to whom this book is dedicated. On his comprehensive experimental work carried out on the famous " Willis " instrument at St. Bees Priory Church and elsewhere, much of its content has been founded.

C. C.
G. D.

October, 1949.

TABLE OF CONTENTS

PREFACE

It may seem the height of presumption for the authors, neither of whom could, by any stretch of imagination, be regarded as a competent organ player, to attempt to deal with Registration. Nevertheless this limitation may have helped them to understand certain aspects of organ playing which may not be familiar to the ordinary organist. It is hoped that they have been able to present these aspects in a way which will be useful and acceptable to both teacher and pupil. Not being restricted to any particular organ, they have studied the most important instruments in this country and some abroad. They have also observed the effects obtained from them by leading players at recitals and under other circumstances. In this way, they have learnt how much, and often how little, the listener actually hears of the effects the player is trying to produce. They have also frequently observed that, while normal teaching will adequately develop manual and pedal technique, phrasing, rhythm, the use of the swell pedal, etc., the general principles of Registration are seldom considered. The pupil learns to register, more or less successfully, certain pieces on the instrument he plays, but he hardly ever seems to have any real understanding as to how to make himself at home on a strange organ. This can only be acquired by a certain amount of study away from the console.

Compared with other players, who can be assured of a fairly standard instrument wherever they may be, the organist is at a disadvantage. Organs of different periods, countries and builders, vary very much—their size varies enormously. It is essential, therefore, that the organist should have a thorough knowledge of the principles underlying the tonal structure of his instrument, in order that he may do full justice to the various types of organs with which he is likely to come in contact. Now, most of the books on the organ are of a technical nature, and consequently of little interest to the average player. This one, however, deals almost entirely with the tonal side of the instrument, and those who wish to study its mechanism in detail must consult standard works on the subject, to which reference will be made in due course.

The present volume is divided into four chapters. An historical account of French and German organs in the eighteenth-century, and French work of the nineteenth-century is given in chapter one. It also includes some introductory remarks on their tonal structure which are necessary for a full understanding of the subject as a whole. This leads up to chapter two, which briefly relates the earlier history of Registration. The historical approach is as necessary to organ playing as it is to most other subjects. Chapter three describes at some length the history of the tonal structure of the modern British organ, explaining the function of its different departments, and the chief variants which obtain. These preliminary chapters lead naturally to chapter four, which deals with the Registration of the modern organ from a novel point of view—that of the listener who, as a rule, gets very little consideration from the great majority of players. Much experimental work with a large number of compositions in various styles, played on different organs, has been taken into account. Observations of the methods used by most of the leading British and foreign organists have also contributed. Some of the recommendations may appear revolutionary, as they cut across long-established traditions. The best suggestion we can offer our readers is : never do anything from blind adherence to habit or custom. Do not be satisfied because your registration sounds well balanced, effective and clear at the console, but get a friend (who need not be an organ expert) to go into the building itself and tell you how much he can distinguish at a distance where the majority of listeners sit. If they are unable to appreciate the effects you are trying to produce, then it is so much wasted effort. In short, endeavour to make your playing and registration as clear *and effective as possible to your audience, for that is of most vital importance.*

It should be mentioned that, while collaboration has been generally maintained throughout the book, one of us (C.C.) is more directly responsible for chapters one and two, while the other (G.D.) has been mainly concerned with chapters three and four. Though we are in complete agreement on matters of principle, which it is our purpose to set out, we naturally do not always see eye to eye on every detail. For instance, we differ somewhat on the merits of organs built before about 1850. Our alternative standpoints appear in parts one and two, respectively. We believe, however, that the usefulness of this book is actually enhanced thereby, since both sides of the argument are presented to the reader, but the principles of Registration which emerge are the same, from whichever viewpoint they are approached.

PART 1—Historical

" He who considers things in their first growth and origin, whether a State or anything else, will obtain the clearest view of them."—Aristotle.

Introductory

A very large proportion of published organ-music was composed before 1750. After that date, there was a lapse of some eighty years or more before much of consequence was again written for the instrument. Those eighty years saw a vital change of outlook in every sphere of art, and after they had elapsed, the kind of organs which began to be built, and the type of music which came to be written for them were entirely different from almost all that had gone before.

Both in quality and quantity, the music of J. S. Bach remains by far the most important contribution made by any great composer to the organist's repertoire. There is also a vast wealth of first-rate music by his lesser contemporaries and predecessors, whose wider recognition would greatly enrich the organ's artistic scope. The total amount of music composed for the organ being comparatively small, so important a part of it can hardly be ignored if the organ is to be taken more seriously by the general musical public. Its wider study is, therefore, not only overdue, but it is also most important that the modern organ should make more adequate provision for its successful performance. As things are, it is seldom possible to produce anything approaching the original effects on a modern organ. But if one understands how a piece was registered, and how it sounded, one can then more readily decide how it may best be treated on a modern instrument.

Unless the organist has a fairly clear mental picture of the type of instrument for which the seventeenth and eighteenth-century composers wrote, it is often impossible for him to realise what effect was originally intended. It is the lack of this knowledge which gives rise to so many unintelligent and unintelligible performances. This particularly applies to the gaily coloured music of the Couperins, and of Daquin, Clérambault, and the other seventeenth and eighteenth-century French composers. It also applies to the wistfully beautiful music of Sweelinck (1562-1621), who was indebted to the genius of the English Tudor masters of the keyboard, and was, in his turn, a powerful influence in Bach's formative years. This music is little known in England, except to discriminating players, because so few have any idea of how it ought to sound.

The departments into which an organ is divided, and the correct apportionment of the stops among them, enable the resources of the instrument to be used to the best advantage. In order that the organist shall be in a position to manage his stops most effectively it is, therefore, important that he should understand why they are so distributed. This applies today with no less force than it did two or three centuries ago, and it is the *raison d'etre* of chapters I and III. They form an almost indispensable introduction to chapters II and IV, respectively.

One can approach the study of early organs in various frames of mind. Some believe that the modern pianoforte and the modern organ are better than anything that came before ; for them, the organs and harpsichords of the eighteenth-century and earlier can possess little more than an antiquarian interest. Others, while admitting the excellence of the modern piano and organ for the rendering of nineteenth and twentieth-century music, feel them to be somewhat lacking when used for the interpretation of the earlier composers. They hold that the eighteenth-century organs and harpsichords were not merely an imperfect and immature edition of their modern successors, but were very important because they were the product of an entirely different musical outlook from that which has prevailed during the last hundred and fifty years. The two viewpoints can be argued *ad nauseam*, and the authors have no intention of discussing the matter here ; each reader must form his own conclusions.

But for the purposes of historical study we shall get more out of the subject if we can approach it with a certain amount of enthusiasm. In Part I it will, therefore, generally be assumed that the early organ gave the early composer what he wanted, and that its design and execution adequately met the needs and taste of those times. He certainly did not envisage anything better. Whether or not this actually was the case is immaterial, but it is a convenient assumption for our purposes. It does not imply that the authors wish to see a return to the organ of the eighteenth-century, and the modern perspective will be restored when we come to Part II.

It has already been stated that this book is not much concerned with the technical or mechanical side of the organ. Yet some knowledge of what goes on inside the instrument is an important requisite in every organist's equipment, and if the reader has not made any study of the subject he is recommended to procure an admirable little book entitled " A Student's Guide to the Organ," by Reginald Whitworth, M.B.E., published by Musical Opinion, London. If he wishes to pursue the subject further, he can study "The Electric Organ," by the same author and publisher.

Another book worthy of study is " The Modern British Organ," by the Rev. Noel A. Bonavia Hunt, M.A., published by A. Weekes & Co. There is also a most informative article on the organ by D. Batigan-Verne (Barrister-at-Law) in the 14th edition of the Encyclopaedia Britannica, which may advantageously be consulted by those who have access to that great work. As the descriptions given in each are so lucid, it is not proposed to deal with the matters contained in them, and the reader will, therefore, be assumed to have an elementary knowledge of the general working principles of the instrument. The organist of a church or other public building with an organ under his care *ought* to possess this much knowledge at least, because those who are financially responsible for the upkeep of the instrument inevitably look to him to advise them about it. It has often happened that, through his ignorance alone, they have been misled, both artistically and economically.

It is significant to reflect that Bach was recognised as probably the foremost organ-building advisory expert of his day in Germany, and he did not consider an intimate knowledge of the instrument's mechanism and design as at all inconsistent with his artistic susceptibilities. His own views on the subject are clearly expressed in a letter recommending Altnikol's appointment as organist at Naumburg, of whom he wrote : " He is . . . fully competent to look after his instrument, qualities requisite in a good organist."

Chapter 1

THE HISTORY OF TONAL DESIGN

The main purpose of this chapter is to describe the schools of organ-building which prevailed in Germany in the eighteenth, and in France in the eighteenth and nineteenth-centuries. As a preliminary, it is necessary to gain some insight into the nature of their main flue and reed choruses, and of the type of Diapason and reed employed.

(1) The Development of the Diapason

There have been three important stages in the development of the Diapason and its chorus. The ancient type of mild and generally flutey Diapason prevailed until the nineteenth century. The transition from the ancient to the modern culminated in the relatively powerful and bright-toned diapason of Edmund Schulze, with its brilliant chorus. This, in turn, led on to the more powerful and foundational English Diapason.

The tonal character of a Diapason pipe is largely determined by the scale, or diameter, of the pipe relative to its length, and by the pressure* and quantity of wind admitted

---

*NOTE : The *quantity* of wind admitted to a pipe is determined by the size of the foothole ; the *pressure* at which it reaches the pipe is determined by the weighting of the reservoirs in which it is stored, on its way from the bellows or blower to the windchest on which stand the pipes. Wind pressure is measured in " inches of water." If any given pressure of air is applied to one end of an open-ended U-tube containing water, the resulting difference in the height of the two columns of water is then a measure of the pressure applied. The pressures mostly employed in organ-building are not very great, a pressure of 3½ inches being equivalent to about two ounces per square inch.

In the eighteenth century, a pressure of between 2½ and 3¼ inches

to it. Light pressures and large scales tend to a flutey quality
of tone, while brilliancy is encouraged by small scales and
heavier pressures. The inter-relationship of these important
factors, and many others in the actual finishing, or voicing,
of the pipes, constitutes the art of the organ-builder.

Whether by choice, or of necessity arising from the
difficulty of raising adequate supplies of wind, the early
organs were very lightly winded. A pressure of 3 inches was
rarely exceeded, and the footholes of the pipes were small,
especially in the basses, though the trebles, which consume
less wind, were often more boldly treated. As a result, the
tone of the early Diapason had three outstanding characteristics :

(a) it was usually more foundational or flutey, and softer
      than modern Diapasons ;

(b) it spoke with remarkable promptitude ;

(c) and owing to the relatively bold trebles it had good
      melodic ability.

This latter attribute is most important if an organ is not
to produce a muddled effect, and many organs of this and the
last century are notably deficient in melodic ability.

The quality of quick speech is pleasing in conjunction
with the fresh, unforced tone of the early Diapasons, though
it would not be pleasant in conjunction with the powerful

---

was usual for all classes of organ stop, though as little as one inch
was employed in small instruments ; 3¼ or 3½ inches was generally
used by Schulze and from 4 inches upwards is usual for the modern
English Diapason. In modern English reed-voicing higher pressures
are employed, about 7 inches being customary for chorus reeds. Tubas
and powerful pedal reeds are commonly voiced on 15 to 20-inch pressure.
A pressure of 50 inches is the greatest actually employed in an English
organ, though 100 inches was at any rate contemplated by Hope-Jones,
and has actually been used in America.

tone of a modern English Diapason. But it is an important aid to clarity when playing polyphonic music. The widespread prevalence of second-rate pneumatic action seems to have dulled the appreciation of many players to the importance of a good attack and release ; yet it is as much a waste of time to try to play Bach's 'D' major Fugue with slow pneumatic action as it is to try to play it in St. Paul's Cathedral or any other over-resonant building. On such actions, effective phrasing is very difficult or even impossible, and variations of touch and accentuation are quite lost.

Many attempts have been made to increase the power of old Diapasons, but almost always with disastrous results. The thin pipe-metal of which they are constructed cannot stand the more vigorous vibrations set up, and an unmusical tone generally results. Where the original manual compass was to GGG, the GGG pipe has often been cut down to CC, so that the scaling is radically altered. One must, therefore, beware of these possible contingencies when listening to what is ostensibly a typical early Diapason. Once encountered, the unforced singing tone of an untouched example can always be distinguished from a stop which has been doctored. The Diapason chorus by Green, on the Great Organ of St. Thomas's Church, Salisbury, is a very fine untouched example.

Gottfried Silbermann was the first transitional builder between the old and the new ; working in the middle of the eighteenth century, he produced a formalised style of instrument, conforming to the rigidly classical taste of the day. His Diapason voicing was markedly bolder than anything earlier, and he used pressures up to $3\frac{1}{4}$ inches for the Hauptwerk, or Great Organ, and as much as 4 inches on the pedals. About a century later his pioneer work was developed almost to finality by another German, Edmund Schulze, though the most characteristic work of the latter was done solely for England.

Schulze did everything to get the maximum power from moderate wind pressures, and most of his Great Organ Diapason choruses are on $3\frac{1}{4}$ or $3\frac{1}{2}$-inch wind. As the scaling he employed was little larger than that of the early builders, the tone of his Diapason was naturally a good deal more brilliant. Increased power was obtained by the use of enormous footholes and a wide mouth. He prevented the tone from becoming strident by the use of adequately heavy pipe metal of fine quality. The tone of a Schulze Diapason is very striking, and his methods were successfully adopted by T. C. Lewis. Schulze did not always employ a powerful unison and his fully developed type is only to be found at Tyne Dock and Leeds parish church.

Modern Diapason voicing has sought a more foundational quality of tone and even greater power, and in a large building such a stop produces a noble and artistically valuable effect. Schulze having reached the useful limits of low-pressure voicing, it was necessary to resort to higher pressures. Unfortunately, on pressures from 4 inches upwards the foothole has to be progressively diminished, so that the gain in power is not proportionate to the increase in pressure. It also becomes increasingly difficult to make the pipe speak reasonably promptly, and other voicing difficulties appear. It was discovered that all these troubles could be overcome by coating the upper lip of the pipe with split skin, when a very prompt-speaking, foundational class of tone resulted. This arrangement was exploited and carried to extremes by Robert Hope-Jones in his " Diapason Phonon," and similar stops. Artistic examples were, however, widely used by Arthur Harrison, generally on between 4 and 6 inch wind, though sometimes less. Harrison's idea was chiefly to eliminate windiness in the copiously blown lower register. Even though leathered, his large Diapasons were often brighter than might be expected, and many competent judges greatly admire the tone quality. The trouble is that, on both tonal and structural grounds, a chorus cannot easily be built up on the leathered Diapason. This did not bother Hope-Jones, who was not interested in chorus-building, but the difficulty remains, and it is unlikely that such stops will long continue to be made. The skilful voicer has since learnt to adopt other remedies. The modern English Diapason is not only impressive in itself, but a foundation upon which a cohesive chorus can be erected.

The modern, the Schulze and the ancient Diapasons are all masterpieces in their several ways. The types of chorus founded on them have different uses, and each may find a place in an entirely complete organ.

(2) The Development of the Diapason Chorus

Having fixed on the style of voicing to be used for the unison Diapason the sort of chorus to be constructed upon it must next be considered. This is primarily a question of the relative power of the different ranks, and the modern and ancient types of chorus must be quite differently proportioned. The size of the building and the position of the organ must also be taken into account.

In the eighteenth-century and before, the chorus was the main consideration, and the 8-ft. stop was merely a part of it, hardly more important than any other rank. In the modern English chorus, the 8-ft. Diapason is the focal point, and everything else is subservient to it. It is, therefore, clear that the two are to be handled quite differently. In some cases, it may be found that they have been mixed up together, and it is then useful to be able to recognise what has happened, dividing the sheep from the goats, as it were, for purposes of registration.

The principal mission in life of the seventeenth and eighteenth-century Diapason chorus was to render polyphonic music with clarity. Homophonic organ music was hardly envisaged, and the accompaniment of congregational singing not much considered. It has just been stated that the 8-ft. Diapason was not regarded as being of outstanding importance in the chorus. Rather was it the intention to produce an effect combining depth with brightness, but in which no individual rank predominated. With this in view, it was usual for all the ranks, Mixtures included, to be practically identical in power.

In general, Mixtures and the artistic use of them have been greatly misunderstood for almost a century, and a correct appreciation of them will be the subject of a good deal of attention throughout this book. It can be said with complete certainty that no successful organ has been made without them. Historically, they are an heritage of the mediaeval vocal organum, or singing in consecutive fifths, the organ copying what was normal choral practice. When strict vocal organum gave way to free-moving parts, and the beginnings of modern harmony appeared, the organ, too, began to be played in harmony, but—quite illogically—it kept its fifth-sounding ranks.

It so happens that the fifth is part of the natural harmonic series of which every musical note is made up, and provided they are suitably voiced, fifth-sounding ranks have an unquestionable reinforcing and cementing effect in a Diapason chorus ; but their artistic value became recognised centuries before it received scientific explanation.

In the beginning, the organ was just one large Mixture, but by degrees (probably in the fourteenth or early fifteenth century) it was found convenient to be able to detach individual ranks from the Mixture, and play them separately. Thus, far from the Mixture being based upon the unison, the latter was, in fact, no more than a part of the Mixture. To make individual ranks separately available either a rudimentary stop-mechanism, or a second keyboard (controlling perhaps the unison alone) could be employed. It was also found convenient to operate the heavy pallets and pallet-springs of the larger pipes by foot rather than by finger, and so, all the essential features of the modern organ gradually appeared.

More and more ranks were detached from the mediaeval Mixture, but today, it is still with us in all its gothic "crudity." Owing to the gradual segregation of the lower pitched ranks, leaving only the higher pitched ranks in the Mixture, the idea has grown up that the sole purpose of a Mixture is to add brilliance. The immensely powerful Mixtures of Schulze also bred the notion that such stops were to be reserved for climaxes only. Mixtures may, indeed, be used in both these ways, and with thrilling effect, especially in large resonant buildings ; though not all musicians appreciate these powerful registers. But in their earlier form, Mixtures were absolutely vital to success, and no one ever thought to question them.

Probably the last prominent writer to state the matter in proper perspective was Dr. E. J. Hopkins, in " Hopkins and Rimbault," the English classic on organ-building, first published in 1855. He said that the purpose of a Mixture was to add point and definition in the bass (where it naturally tended to be absent) and weight and substance in the treble. To achieve this, a number of " breaks " was necessary, and these are the very essence of the true chorus Mixture. Some modern writers have decried breaks as the downfall of the Mixture, and insofar as they are willing to allow it a grudged survival, it is only in a form that permits the minimum number of breaks. In so doing, they show how imperfectly they understand the matter.

If one plays on 8-ft. and 4-ft. Diapasons of fairly foundational quality, in the bottom octave of the keyboard, the tone is " woolly " and lacking in clarity. If, to increase the power, one were to duplicate the 8-ft. and 4-ft. pipes, the cost in large pipes and wind supply would be great, and the artistic gain would be slight. Both on practical and artistic grounds it would be better to add high-pitched quint and unison ranks—for example, unisons sounding a 15th, 22nd, and 29th above the 8-ft. and quints sounding a 12th, 19th, and 26th above the 8-ft. If it were practicable to carry these ranks up to the top of the keyboard, they would degenerate into a series of indeterminate squeals, finally fading into merciful inaudibility. The top pipe would be impracticably small, as its speaking length would be only $\frac{3}{16}$ of an inch, and it would be impossible to tune. Once again, then, both on practical and artistic grounds, it is desirable to break back the ranks so that at the top of the compass in a five-rank quint Mixture, the lowest rank is in unison with the 8-ft. rank, and the remainder sound a fifth, octave, twelfth and fifteenth above it. To bridge this gap inconspicuously it is desirable that only one rank should break back at a time and there will, thus, be four breaks in all, probably one at each 'C.' What happens is that where the 8-ft. and 4-ft. stops rise five octaves in pitch, the Mixture only rises three octaves. It thus exactly performs the mission required of it in "Hopkins and Rimbault." The breaks may be managed so as to be almost indistinguishable, and the chorus is enriched at a minimum outlay of pipe-metal and wind. It is indeed seldom that the dictates of art and expediency are found in such convenient accord!

In France, the mediaeval notion of the Mixture being the centre of importance died so hard that as late as 1770 Dom Bédos, in his monumental "L'Art du Facteur d'orgues," remarks that the "Plein Jeu" is "nourished" by the separate foundation stops. So true is this that one may play upon ten, fifteen, or more ranks of 18th-century French Mixtures with no greater "nourishment" than a solitary stopped Flute or a Diapason of soft intonation. Yet the effect is less brilliant and powerful than a mere three ranks of Schulze Mixture work; but it is fresher.*

---

* COMPOUND STOP NOMENCLATURE. Properly speaking, the term "Mixture" should be restricted to such compound stops as have been so far described, comprising quints and unisons only. The term "Fourniture" is similarly appropriate to quint Mixtures of several ranks of high pitch and it has good historical authority. For still higher pitched stops, the term "Cymbal" or "Sharp Mixture" is correct and these sometimes repeat every octave. The "Sesquialtera" had originally two ranks only, comprising the 12th and 17th, but in English organs the term has been misappropriated to include any breaking Mixture (usually 17 - 19 - 22 at CC) containing a tierce. The term "Harmonics" was applied by Messrs. Harrison and Harrison to a compound stop which they revived in this country (though they did not actually introduce it) containing the flat twenty-first, or septième, as well as the tierce, quint and unison. The term "Cornet" has also been loosely applied, and it will be discussed later. It would save much confusion if this terminology were more closely adhered to, and "compound stop" rather than "Mixture" were used generically. Other fancy names have been used to describe compound stops, but they are of little importance. Those named in this footnote include all the principal varieties.

So far, we have only considered compound stops containing quint and unison ranks, but in late times the other constituents of the harmonic series* have been added.

These are the 17th, flat 21st, and even the 23rd above the unison. Such stops partake more of the nature of timbre creators rather than of chorus Mixtures, and as such, it is logical that breaks should be minimised. They form a useful foil to the quint Mixtures, and Messrs. Harrison almost invariably include an example of each in their Great organs when possible. They are labelled " Mixture " and " Harmonics," respectively, the composition at bottom C being, 15, 19, 22, 26, 29 and (12, 15) 17, 19, ♭21, 22, the 12th and 15th of the Harmonics drawing separately, in the usual manner. The Harmonics are usually carried up 43 notes before the break is introduced, so that the stop is also available in solo combinations.

Quint, tierce, and seventh-sounding ranks may also be made independently available on separate stops, when they are commonly called " Mutations." They greatly assist the smooth build-up of the chorus, and they may be employed to " colour " it in a number of different ways which are most valuable. Such stops may also be used melodically, in conjunction with one or more unison stops. They are then known as " *solo* Mutations," and they formed an all-important part of the " solo " effects of early organs. Such solo Mutations are generally softer and more flutey than chorus Mutations, and though the line of demarcation is not now so sharp, the early builders and organists kept the two most sedulously segregated for purposes of registration. Sometimes, a solo

---

* Taking the unison as 1, the first three octaves of the harmonic series are 8, 12, 15, 17, 19, ♭21, 22, having wavelengths $\frac{1}{2}$, $\frac{1}{3}$, $\frac{1}{4}$, $\frac{1}{5}$, $\frac{1}{6}$, $\frac{1}{7}$ and $\frac{1}{8}$, respectively, of the unison.

stop might have more than one rank, a favourite in Germany
being the " Sesquialtera," which originally, and properly,
denoted a two-rank solo register sounding the 12th and 17th
throughout. Almost every organ (especially in France and
England) had a solo " Cornet," which was generally mounted
on a separate sound-board (whence the term " Mounted
Cornet ") and consisted of a stopped unison and large-scale,
lightly-winded open ranks sounding the octave, twelfth,
fifteenth and seventeenth. The tone, as far as it can be
described, was piquant, full and reedy. There is a fine
specimen by Schulze at Doncaster Parish Church (1862)
and another by Lewis at Southwark Cathedral (1897), but
these are more boldly voiced than the seventeenth and
eighteenth-century examples. Among others, Messrs.
Compton are again using the cornet in modernised form. In
their important instrument in the *B.B.C. Studio at Maida
Vale, London, there is an extended unit furnishing Cornets
of 32-ft., 16-ft. and 8-ft. pitches. Two are on the Great, of
which one reinforces the 8-ft. series, much as did the classical
prototype just described. The other is pitched an octave
lower, reinforcing the 16-ft. series. The 8-ft. Cornet makes a
fine solo stop, and both it and the 16-ft. Cornet can also be
used as chorus stops, when they immensely enrich and
colour the ensemble, which also comprises two quint chorus
Mixtures. On the pedals, there are Cornets of 16-ft. and
32-ft. pitches, of which the latter is a most admirable substitute for a small 32-ft. reed. It will thus be seen that tone-
building by means of solo Mutations has much to be said for
it, and the subject will frequently be referred to later. When

---

* Further details of this instrument will be found towards the end
of chapter III. The Compton Cornet incorporates many partials not
used in the eighteenth-century, including the 9th, 11th, 13th, 15th,
17th and 19th, of which the two latter sound more than three octaves
higher than the fundamental.

the wide range of tone colours made practicable by modern voicing methods came into existence it was, perhaps, natural that solo Mutations should wane, and for a time they practically disappeared. Nowadays, it is again becoming increasingly recognised that each kind of solo effect has its own proper sphere of utility, and Mutations are once more appearing in such modern organs in this country as make any pretence at completeness. The firm of Willis must be given credit for their early re-introduction and exploitation in this country from 1925 onwards. Not only are solo Mutations found valuable in the performance of much modern music, but in the rendering of music of the seventeenth and eighteenth-centuries it is no over-statement to say that they are indispensable.

Summing up the eighteenth-century Diapason chorus: It consisted of a relatively large number of ranks of slight power and more or less flutey tone. It relied largely upon its numerous Mixtures, which, nevertheless, did not, when properly treated, produce an effect of overwhelming brilliance. All ranks were of practically identical power, and the 8-ft. pitch was given no special predominance, although it was powerfully reinforced by the resultant tone precipitated by the Mixtures. It may be epitomised by quoting the Grand orgue in the instrument built for the church of St. Sulpice, Paris, by Clicquot, in 1781. The complete instrument possessed five manuals and pedals and a total of 63 speaking stops. The copious chorus, Mixture and solo Mutation ranks, of all pitches, in conjunction with a minimum of 8-ft. registers, clearly shows the logical development of the eighteenth-century flue chorus. The presence of a stop of 32-ft. pitch on the manuals is remarkable, though it was by no means unique ; Paris possessed another in the organ at Nôtre

Dame, where the Grand Orgue also comprised the important 5⅓-ft. Quint, which was somewhat unaccountably omitted at St. Sulpice.

	ft.		ft.
*Montre ...	32	°Tierce ...	1⅗
Montre ...	16	°Larigot ...	1⅓
Bourdon ...	16	°Cornet ...	V
Montre ...	8	Grosse Fourniture	VI
Bourdon ...	8	Petite Fourniture...	IV
Prestant ...	4	Cymbale ...	IV
°Flute ...	4	1re Trompette ...	8
°Gross Tierce ...	3⅕	2me Trompette ...	8
°Nazard ...	2⅔	1re Clairon ...	4
Doublette	2	2me Clairon ...	4
°Quarte de Nazard	2	Voix humaine ...	8

The stops marked ° are the " Jeux de Mutation " or solo mutation series. The remainder of the fluework constitutes the "Plein Jeu" or Diapason chorus. This differentiation will be further discussed in chapter II.

Silbermann worked on largely similar lines, but his voicing was more brilliant and powerful. It has already been explained that his work led on to the English organs of Schulze, from 1851 onwards. The tonal quality of Schulze's Diapasons has also been described—very much bolder, and considerably richer in harmonic development than any earlier work, and reaching the maximum power that can artistically be attained on light pressure wind. For his chorus, Schulze continued the early precedent of making all the ranks of identical power. In his Mixtures, he generally made breaks of a whole octave (i.e., two ranks at a time), with the result that they are very noticeable. In the whole of the upper

---

* FRENCH STOP NOMENCLATURE. The Montre and Prestant approximate to our Open Diapason and Principal. Other terms are explained in the text.

half of the manual, the composition of a Schulze five-rank Mixture was 1, 5, 8, 12, 15, so that it produced, in effect, a supplemental Great to Fifteenth, superimposed on the normal one. Now, while the ear is apparently able to enjoy quite powerful musical sounds around 8-ft. pitch, it becomes very sensitive to great power in the higher register. The full Diapason chorus of a Schulze Great can be taken only in small doses, and many people cannot take it at all. In a large, resonant building, however, the effect is indeed most thrilling. The Schulze chorus, therefore, made it clear that, while the system of having all the ranks of equal power was quite satisfactory when they were fairly soft, it was not so successful when the power of the ranks was substantially increased; and when the large modern Diapason came into use, this process of chorus building became inapplicable. It was, therefore, logical to step down the power of its upper-work. Thus, the 4-ft. is softer than the 8-ft., the 2-ft. softer still, and the Twelfth even further reduced. Nevertheless, the upperwork may still be of considerable power, the Mixture adding a sensible degree of climax.

Such a Diapason chorus will not, however, be an ideal medium for playing polyphonic music, as its pronounced 8-ft. bias will make it too ponderous and thick for the detail to be heard; it is essentially an ensemble for broad, massed effects, and the support of congregational singing.

Some builders make their second Diapason fairly bright in tone, and only a trifle softer than the 4-ft. stop. In this way, the upperwork can be based upon either or both unison at will, according to the type and period of music to be played. This is a very good arrangement for organs and buildings of the middle size. Sometimes, one immense unison Diapason is added to a complete, light pressure, old-style chorus. This stop, possibly admirable in itself, and most useful when a big unison effect is required, will entirely destroy the balance if it is added to the rest of the chorus. Where such an arrangement obtains, it must be used with the necessary selective discrimination, and it would really be better if such stops were placed on the Solo manual, quite separate from the Great Organ.

It therefore emerges that the old type of chorus is ideal for polyphonic and other early music, while the modern chorus is invaluable in modern music and for the accompaniment of congregational singing. A special feature of the modern chorus is that it provides the organist with a *forte* without having recourse to any reeds. A variety of *forte* effects is a most important attribute of the modern organ, if players would only take advantage of it. So it seems that, in large organs, where the Great would contain 15 stops or more, the ideal arrangement is to divide it up into two parts, one of which may, at will, be transferred to another manual for purpose of contrast. In this way, both the old and modern style of chorus can be simultaneously represented. It will be seen that each type of chorus is entirely self-contained, and requires no assistance from chorus reeds, which need not form any essential part of the modern Great Organ. This idea will be further developed in Part II. For the moment, the historical development of the organ's main flue chorus has been followed out in sufficient detail, and we can now pass on to the reed chorus, which, though secondary, is still of vital importance.

(3) The Development of the Reed Chorus

In the first place, what is a *chorus reed*? Is it a stop which will " blend " with the Diapason chorus, or is it one which will form the basis of a satisfactory reed chorus, independent of flue support ?

Now, " blend " is a very elusive quality, and the more one considers it, the more one sees that it is very largely a matter of taste. In the ultimate, it is what appears to be a " good effect," and this will naturally depend on conditions, and vary with the individual listener. Assuming that reeds *can* be used with Diapasons to good effect, it may be argued, with equal force, that the best type of reed for the purpose is (*a*) thin and fiery, (*b*) smooth and close ! The fact of the matter is that reed and Diapason tone will not combine at all well, though it is true that reeds can be used to colour a Diapason chorus, and add a certain intensity without swamping it. But such reeds may be of almost any shade of tone quality provided they are not so powerful as to overwhelm the flue-work and in the unlikely event of their being in tune with it. When we use powerful reeds in the Tuba class, coupled for climax effects, let us be honest, and admit that any question of " blend " disappears ; the brass is overwhelming, and the Diapason chorus is left as a poor " also-ran."

From this point of view, therefore, we are not likely to get very far in defining a chorus reed, and it seems as though we may do better if we look for the class of tone which will best compound a reed chorus of 16-ft., 8-ft and 4-ft. registers to be effective alone, without flue backing, except, perhaps, to the extent of a brilliant compound stop. This is, indeed, the tendency of the modern Swell Organ, in which the fluework contributes little or nothing to the reed chorus.

Such, too, was the case in the seventeenth and eighteenth-century French organ, so that the wheel has turned full circle. It was only in the nineteenth-century in this country that our generally inferior light pressure reeds were considered to need support by the fluework.

Once again, therefore, the historical approach is indicated, and we find that England, and Germany (except as to the Pedal Organ), can be summarily dismissed as non-starters, for the builders of neither country envisaged the possibility of a complete chorus of manual reed tone. How far English organists of the eighteenth century ever drew their Trumpets with the fluework is rather doubtful, and it is also difficult to assess the merits of early English Trumpets, since so few of them have survived in anything like their original condition. Such evidence as exists suggests that, judged by the standards of their day, they were quite good, being probably softer and more refined in tone than the French pattern. The Germans did not supply many chorus reeds on the manuals, but they largely relied upon them for definition in the Pedal, where they appeared in 32ft., 16ft., 8ft., 4ft., and even 2-ft. pitches, to support the manual flue choruses.

But in France, we find the problem of the genuine reed chorus being tackled to some purpose at an early date, certainly by the mid-seventeenth-century. The early French school of organ-building began to take shape in the latter half of the sixteenth century, and continued an unbroken course of development until its complete cessation at the French revolution. It attained its zenith in the work of François-Henri Clicquot in the third quarter of the eighteenth-century, although the school had reached its purest and most virile stage a century earlier.

The construction of the organ beating reed somewhat resembles its orchestral, single-reed prototype. But in the organ, the player's mouth is replaced by the boot of the pipe. The tone of the stop is largely determined by the length, thickness, and curvature of the brass reed tongue, the shape and size of the shallot opening (which the reed successively covers and uncovers in the course of its vibration), the shapes and scale of the tube, or resonator, and the wind pressure. The length and thickness of the tongue, relative to the pitch of the pipe, is largely determined by the wind pressure, and Clicquot and his contemporaries almost invariably worked on a pressure of $2\frac{1}{2}$ inches. This is very close to the absolute minimum upon which it is practicable to voice a reed. So light a pressure can set only a very thin reed in motion, and the thinner the reed, the longer it has to be, to vibrate at any given frequency. Such a reed produces a very thin, intense quality of tone ; it also affords an exceedingly rapid attack, the like of which is hardly to be found in England. The fiery quality of tone is further enhanced by the shallot, which is open and parallel sided. Such " body " as the tone possesses is attributable to the fairly wide scale of the resonators.

So intense is the tone, that at first hearing it may even strike the hearer as harsh. The French aptly describe it as " trés nette," but although the term seems almost self-explanatory, there is no adequate English equivalent. It is not inept to say that the difference between a Clicquot and a Willis reed is very much the same as the difference between a Ruckers harpsichord and a modern Steinway grand pianoforte. Those who admire the harpsichord will also like the Clicquot reed ; but others may not appreciate it.

Unlike the modern chorus reed, it was not intended that the French stops would be used with the fluework. This may seem odd, but there were good reasons for it. In the first place, there was the question of wind supply. When the French divided their organs into three watertight compartments—the " Plein Jeu " or Diapason chorus, the "Jeux de

Mutation," and the reeds—there is little doubt that it was the wind supply difficulty, as well as artistic aims, which they had in mind. Secondly, it is an inherent weakness of the light pressure reeds that they are easily affected by changes of temperature and other disturbing influences ; they are, therefore, very seldom in tune with the fluework. Thirdly, the logically minded French did not like the hybrid mixture of sounds which resulted from combining the reed and flue choruses ; the reeds spoilt the freshness of the fluework, and the fluework detracted from the intensity of the reeds. The only flue stops generally drawn with the reeds were a 4-ft. Principal or a short compass Cornet, to cover any irregularities in the reeds, while the Cornet helped to keep up the power in the treble—always a difficulty in light-pressure reed-voicing. To show how far the French segregated their reeds, the third manual of the St. Sulpice instrument, of which the Grand Orgue has already been quoted, contained only the following four stops :—

			ft.
Bombarde	...	...	16
Trompette	...	...	8
Clairon	...	...	4
Cornet	...	...	V

and several such departments existed elsewhere, a remarkable instance being the Bombarde clavier in the small five-manual organ of the Couperins at St. Gervais, Paris, which contains only one stop, a 16-ft. Bombarde.

We had to wait a century before anything so complete as the St. Sulpice Clavier des Bombardes was to be found in England.

Apart from the intensity of tone, the attack and release are qualities no less striking. These can be appreciated to the full in conjunction with well-made tracker action, whose sensitiveness to touch cannot be equalled, even by electric action, though the other advantages of electric action are overwhelming. The attack is absolutely startling ; the note really comes on with a " smack." For the adequate performance of early French music, nothing less is really adequate. A complete chorus of such stops, whether one likes the tone quality or not, is an achievement to be reckoned with, and it can certainly fulfil the requirement of being able to stand alone without flue support. It is, of course, as unsuited to the requirements of modern music as is the harpsichord to the music of Chopin. It also has the inherent disadvantage of instability, and a very limited range of power and quality, so that little allowance could be made for the size and acoustics of different buildings.

In nineteenth-century France, Cavaillé-Coll successfully developed the eighteenth-century technique, usually employing a pressure of 3½ inches for the bass, and 5 inches for the treble part of the compass, and making the trebles double length or " harmonic." His reeds are practically a more powerful edition of their eighteenth-century predecessors, continuing to employ thin, unweighted tongues and open, parallel shallots.

In England, attempts to develop light-pressure reed voicing were generally less successful and often ended with a harsh, rasping sort of tone, overpowerful, rattling basses, and thin wheezing trebles. William Hill made the first attempts at exploiting considerably higher pressures, in 1839, at Birmingham Town Hall, where he added a solo reed on 11-inch wind. The technique, however, was not fully mastered until Henry Willis and his brother George astounded the organ world by their immense, and still unsurpassed, instrument installed at St. George's Hall, Liverpool, in 1855. This organ was surely the greatest single step forward in organ-building that the world has ever witnessed. In 1867 began the development of loaded reeds on heavy pressure wind by Henry's gifted son Vincent, who, at Best's instigation, raised the pressure of the four solo Tubas at St. George's Hall from $9\frac{1}{2}$ to 22 inches, with stupendous effect.

The increased pressure of wind enabled thicker and shorter tongues to be employed, with brass weights attached to them. Double-length or harmonic tubes were used in the middle and upper registers of the Willis Tuba. This method of construction made it possible to obtain great power without the least blatancy, and the reliability and stability of Willis reeds, thus ensured, has never been surpassed, being now proverbial. Willis did make a number of successful chorus reeds on $3\frac{1}{2}$-inch wind, with unweighted tongues, but his most characteristic work was his superb chorus of 16-ft., 8-ft. and 4-ft. Trumpets and Cornopeans on 7-inch wind, and solo and pedal reeds on 15-inch pressure or more. The shallot opening was reduced, being V-shaped and coming to a stop somewhat short of the fixed end of the reed. This further refined the tone, but Willis never carried refinement to the point that his reeds lost the virile quality and that brilliant " clang-tint " which has sometimes been lost by later builders. Insofar as reeds can be used effectively with fluework, the Willis type is most suitable. It is, however, at its best when used alone, and a chorus of 16-ft., 8-ft., and 4-ft. reeds by Vincent Willis is an effect of unsurpassed splendour. The relation of Willis's reeds to his Great Organ Diapason chorus will be discussed in chapter III. Later voicers have produced much greater variety of tone, but as chorus-builders, the Willis reeds are unrivalled.

If they were in any way inferior to the light pressure Clicquot reed at its best, it was in the matter of attack, and it is interesting that in the latest work of the John Compton Organ Company, and one or two other progressive voicers, something of the attack and intensity of the Clicquot reed has been combined with the reliability and refinement of the Willis type. In this way, a complete general purpose reed has been produced.

Now that we have briefly traced the historical development of the different types of Diapason and Trumpet, and the various kinds of Diapason and reed chorus, we can turn to considering the early organ as a whole.

(4) The Seventeenth and Eighteenth-Century German Organ

The last great representative of this school was Gottfried Silbermann, who flourished in the second quarter of the eighteenth-century ; but it was more typically represented by Arp Schnitger, whose best work was done half-a-century earlier. The eighteenth-century was a time of rigid art-forms, and this is reflected in the austere specifications of Silbermann organs. The seventeenth-century was a time of experiment and change, and the tempestuous chromaticisms and sharp contrasts of the music of some of the early seventeenth-century composers—notably Monteverdi and our English Dowland and John Bull—often seem strangely akin to the present-day outlook. This is reflected in the Schnitger organ, which presents a wealth of subtlety in registration that is not available on a Silbermann. Furthermore, although Bach did play on Silbermann instruments, he was more familiar for most of his life with the north-German Schnitger school, which is also more appropriate to Buxtehude,

Sweelinck, and the earlier composers. Schnitger built some very large four-manual organs of 60 speaking stops or more, but for our purposes it will perhaps be less confusing to consider a smaller instrument.

A good example is at Steinkirchen (a village about 20 miles from Hamburg) which is very complete despite possessing only 28 speaking stops. Commenced the year that Bach was born, it remains in its original condition having recently undergone a skilful and reverent restoration by Herr von Beckerath.

STEINKIRCHEN. SCHNITGER: 1685-7.

*HAUPTWERK		*OBERWERK		*PEDAL	
	ft.		ft.		ft.
Quintatön ...	16	Gedackt ...	8	Principal ...	16
Principal ...	8	Rohrflöte ...	4	Oktave ...	8
Rohrflöte ...	8	Quinte ...	2⅔	Oktave ...	4
Oktave ...	4	Oktave ...	2	Nachthorn ...	2
Nasat	2⅔	Spitzflöte ...	2	Rauschquint ...	II
Oktave... ...	2	Tertian ...	II	Mixtur... ...	IV
Gemshorn ...	2	Scharf	III-V	Posaune ...	16
Mixture	IV-VI	Krumphorn	8	Trompete ...	8
Cymbel ...	III			Kornett ...	2
Sesquialtera ...	II				
Trompete ...	8	Tremulant			
		Manual Coupler			
		Tracker Action.		2¾-inch wind	

* NOMENCLATURE OF GERMAN MANUAL DEPARTMENTS. The German names for the different manual departments were somewhat elastic in application, often being determined more by their location in the instrument than by their tonal characteristic. In some instruments, for example (as in Bach's own organ at Arnstadt), the Oberwerk operated as the Great, but here it is more in the nature of a Choir Organ, and the Hauptwerk, as is normal, is the Great. The Oberwerk in its most typical form, has been likened to a reed-less Swell, while

It is apparent that three well developed flue choruses
form the basis of the organ; each department is entirely
complete in itself and independent of couplers. The Germans
had the same three types of stop already mentioned in connection with the French organ, but their organists were
not so particular about them as the French. It may appear
strange that each manual department contains two 2-ft.
stops and only one 4-ft., but the reason becomes apparent
if one divides the upperwork of each as follows:—

	Chorus Upperwork		*Solo Mutations*	
		ft.		*ft.*
HAUPTWERK ...	Oktave ...	2	Nasat ...	2⅔
	Mixture ...	IV-VI	Gemshorn ...	2
	Cymbel ...	III	Sesquialtera	
			(12, 17)	II
OBERWERK ...	Quinte ...	2⅔	Spitzflöte ...	2
	Oktave ...	2	Tertian	
	Scharf ...	III-V	(17, 19)	II

Either of these "pinnacles" could be added at will to
the 16-ft., 8-ft., and 4-ft. "main structure" of each department. The Oberwerk foundation is composed of stopped
Flutes, 8-ft. and 4-ft.; it has no Diapason below 2-ft. pitch.
This looks rather alarming, but when it is remembered that

---

the Brustwerk or Ruckpositiv approximated to the Choir Organ.
Silbermann, who never exceeded three manuals, described his various
departments as follows:—

Hauptmanual :	Von grossen und gravitatischen mensuren.
Oberwerk :	Von scharffen und penetranten mensuren.
Brustwerk :	Von delikaten und lieblichen mensuren.
Pedal :	Von starken und durch dringenden mensuren.

the Diapasons (*i.e.*, the Principals and Oktaves) are no louder than the Flutes, and are themselves on the foundational side, the idea no longer seems so illogical. The power of the Oberwerk is, indeed, a little softer than the Hauptwerk, but the contrast is nothing like so great as exists, for example, between the full Great Diapason chorus and the Swell Diapason chorus in an English organ. The contrast is more of quality than of quantity ; it is sufficiently marked to be useful, but not so violent as to sever the continuity of a composition by a change of manual. It must be remembered that there were no swell-boxes with which to gloss over manual changes, as we are now accustomed to hear. The Quintatön is a very valuable sub-unison in conjunction with a softly-voiced diapason chorus of this kind. Its pronounced overtones ensure that, while it adds depth, there is no muddiness. Even in larger early German organs, possessing open 16-ft. manual stops, they are of very soft but clear intonation. It was one of the primary aims of the seventeenth and eighteenth-century continental builders to secure this quality of depth without thickness in their Great Organs. In England this was not, unfortunately, the case, as manual doubles were virtually unknown ; our organs were, however, characterised by an excellence of refinement and finish seldom encountered on the continent. In modern times, the thick, dense tonal quality of many Diapasons makes them unsuitable for the rendering of polyphonic music ; yet we do not want to dispense with them, as they have other important uses. So that the only possible solution lies in the divided Great, already mentioned, and to be further discussed in chapter III.

At Steinkirchen there is no pedal coupler and none is needed. Aided by the two Mixtures (19, 22, and 26, 29, 33, 36, respectively) full Pedal fluework is perfectly matched with Hauptwerk up to Mixture, but to it may be added the 8-ft. Trompete for improved definition, especially in rapid passages. When the Cymbel is drawn, or the Oberwerk coupled to Hauptwerk, the Pedal Posaune is also needed. The balance is then perfect and the reeds add that punch and definition which nothing else can do. Of moderate power, Schnitger reeds are less fiery and intense than the contemporary French examples; but they are no less successful. The Germans quite often included a 2-ft. pedal reed before the 4-ft., but it was regarded as a solo rather than as a chorus register, though it could also be used to add point to full Pedal.

In larger organs of the Schnitger class, greater variety would naturally be found, and the character of the different manual departments was obtained by contrasted tone families. The small scale, colourful Quintatöns contrasted with large scale, sombre Gedackts. Open wood Flutes, such as Hohlflöte and Waldflöte, are found in all pitches and also half-stopped pipes (Rohrflöte), as well as the tapered Spitzflöte. Solo reeds are more plentifully provided, often in 16-ft. pitch. The Germans were also fond of reeds with short resonators of varied and remarkable shape, known as "Schnarrwerk." Their instability, and strangely buzzing tone are not generally acceptable to modern ears, but they do suggest that Bach would have found plenty of use for our modern solo reeds.

The Schnitger and Silbermann organs are much prized in Germany, and religiously preserved without alteration. They also find many enthusiastic English-speaking adherents, among whom an American, the Hon. Senator Emerson Richards, is prominent. It is interesting to know his outlook on these instruments, and, writing (in " The American Organist ") of another Schnitger organ at Stade, near Steinkirchen, he has described its effect as follows : " Full organ fills the rather large church with a flood of pure tone— no rumble or muddiness. Bach . . . came out with an entirely new meaning. A precise, bell-like tone, rich in harmonics, but characterised by a lightness and transparency, gave an interest to the music never achieved by the romantic organ to which we are accustomed. There is plenty of power ; the Mixtures are responsible for that ; but it is a different kind of power. After becoming accustomed to it one never has the same interest in chorus reeds as instruments of power." His words are remarkably reminiscent of those used by the great English player W. T. Best, in a letter to the College of Organists (not as yet Royal) in 1881, when he wrote : " It is particularly necessary to urge the extreme importance of Mixture-work, artistically tempered and of melodious sonority. No other legitimate means exist, nor can ever exist, of adding harmonious power to an organ."

(5) The Seventeenth and Eighteenth-Century French Organ

The French organ reached something like standardisation towards the end of the sixteenth-century, and it continued with little more than minor refinement until its cessation at the time of the French Revolution, two centuries later. It is generally held to have reached its purest and most vigorous development about midway in the reign of Louis XIV. A typical example of this period was the instrument at St. Spire, Corbeil, Ile de France, built by G. Joly in 1675, containing three manuals and 28 speaking stops.

	Plein Jeu	Mutations	Reeds
	ft.	ft.	ft.
GRAND ORGUE 16 Stops	Bourdon .. 16 Bourdon .. 8 Montre ... 8 Prestant .. 4 Doublette 2 Fourniture IV Cymbale .. III	Flûte ... 4 Nazard ... 2⅔ Quarte de Nazard .. 2 Tierce ... 1⅗ Flageolet . 1 Cornet ... V	Trompette 8 Clairon ... 4 Voix Humaine 8
POSITIF 8 Stops	Bourdon .. 8 Montre ... 4 Doublette 2 Fourniture III Cymbale .. II	Nazard ... 2⅔ Larigot ... 1⅓	Cromorne 8
ECHO 2 Stops Short Compass	—	Cornet ... V	Voix Humaine 8
PEDALE 2 Stops 29 Notes	Flûte ... 8	—	Trompette 8

At the end of this period, more doubles began to be introduced, and also Mutations of the 16-ft. series (5⅓ ft. and 3⅕ ft.); 16-ft. manual reeds, and the " Clavier des Bombardes " of the kind already mentioned, also appeared. The remarkably truncated Pedal Organ of Corbeil never really grew up, and only in the largest and latest instruments did the Pédale possess 16-ft. registers.

As in the case of the German organ, interest centres round the two very fully developed manual flue choruses of the

Grand Orgue and Positif. Once again, the contrast between them exists, but it is not exaggerated. The most marked difference is in the pitch, the Grand Orgue having an 8-ft., and the Positif a 4-ft. foundation. The tone of the early French flue chorus is markedly foundational ; even more so than the equivalent German or English choruses. The Bourdons, too, are of very large scale and sombre tone, though devoid of " thickness." The Germans certainly used such variety of voicing as was known to them, and they even attempted rudimentary string tone. The French allowed no such variety ; nor did their highly formalised system of registration demand it. They were content with such effects as they could obtain by combining their solo Mutations with the foundation stops ; they also had the Cornet, Trompette, Voix Humaine and Cromorne. The Cromorne was the predecessor of the modern organ Clarinet, and, like it, had half-length, cylindrical resonators. It differed in being of larger scale and having open shallots. The tone is brilliant, being less full and " woody " than the modern Clarinet, so that it can be used as a solo or chorus register. There are still a few successful examples to be found in England, but the Clicquot variety is best.

It was soon discovered that it would be convenient to have such solo stops as the Trompette and Cornet available on a separate manual, thus avoiding changes of stops, for which there were no facilities in the eighteenth-century. So the Récit and Echo manuals came into use. Their stops were mostly required for solo purposes, and it was therefore considered unnecessary for them to be of full compass. Accordingly, they stopped short at some note between Tenor and Middle C.

Throughout its pre-revolution career, the French Pédale

remained an inconsiderable adjunct ; hardly more than a solo department, as in the example quoted. The French organ was therefore but little better equipped for the performance of Bach's music than was the contemporary English instrument, which had no pedals at all ; nor was the French instrument helped out by long manuals and manual to pedal couplers. Manual couplers were rare, but there was usually a somewhat clumsy arrangement for coupling the Positif to the Grand Orgue. The stop-knobs were most promiscuously grouped, and had a tremendous length of draw, so that changes of registration were difficult to effect without the aid of an assistant.

(6) The Nineteenth and Twentieth-Century French Organ

After the French Revolution, the French organ lay dormant for a time, and it was not until the appearance of Aristide Cavaillé-Coll that new development took place. Starting work about 1840, he dominated the French scene until nearly the end of the century. Like his great English contemporary, Henry Willis, he owed little to his predecessors, and struck out an entirely new style of his own.

For his flue chorus, he abandoned the eighteenth-century " montre flûtée," and built upon an entirely heterogeneous foundation. The 8-ft. registers of a typical Cavaillé-Coll Grand Orgue consisted of a Montre, Gambe, Flûte Harmonique and Bourdon. The Montre was of somewhat thin, unsubstantial tone, not unlike some middle-period Willis Diapasons. The Gambe had little trace of true string tone, and approximated to an English Geigen. All four 8-ft. stops were of moderate power, and voiced with a view to good blending ability ; they therefore combined quite well. Cavaillé-Coll reeds are of considerable power, extreme brilliance, excellent attack and good regulation. In a large, resonant building their effect is most striking, but under less favourable circumstances they appear uncongenial and strident to most English ears. In his solo Strings and Flutes he attained effects full of colour. Although he generally included a solo Cornet, he often omitted solo Mutations, especially in his early period, and until he was influenced by Guilmant and other scholarly artists ; the remarkably complete series at Nôtre Dame, Paris, is exceptional. His pedal fluework is mild, even the largest instruments possessing only three 16-ft. stops ; a lightly-blown open wood Flute, a mild String or " Contrebasse " and the conventional Bourdon. His pedal reeds, by contrast, are immensely telling. His stop-apportionment varied so greatly that it is practically impossible to select any one instrument which can be regarded as typical. The specimen chosen for reproduction here is the famous instrument at the Church of Saint-Clotilde, Paris, of which César Franck was organist from the time of its completion, in 1859, until 1890, the date of his death. This is a good example of a Cavaillé-Coll specification, and has more upperwork than many. It does, however, lack the usual solo Cornet. The Cavaillé-Coll Récit was seldom more fully developed than this one, except in his largest and later instruments. To some extent, the old relationship of Grand Orgue and Positif remain. Its most unusual feature is the presence of two 16-ft. reeds and only one 16-ft. flue stop on the Pédale. In nearly all his other instruments the place of the Basson would be taken by a Bourdon, or " Soubasse." The total number of speaking stops is 46, the manual compass CC-f3 (54 notes) and the pedal compass CCC-D (27 notes).

GRAND ORGUE 14 *Stops*		POSITIF 14 *Stops*		RECIT EXPRESSIF 10 *Stops*	
	ft.		ft.		ft.
Montre	16	Bourdon	16	Bourdon	8
Bourdon	16	Montre	8	Flûte	
Montre	8	Gambe	8	Harmonique	8
Gambe	8	Flûte		Viole de Gambe	8
Flûte		Harmonique	8	Voix Céleste	8
Harmonique	8	Bourdon	8	Flûte Octaviante	4
Bourdon	8	Salicional	8	Octavin	2
Prestant	4	Prestant	4	Basson-Hautbois	8
Octave	4	Flûte Octa-		Voix Humaine	8
Quinte	2⅔	viante	4	Trompette	8
Doublette	2	Quinte	2⅔	Clairon	4
Plein Jeu	—	Doublette	2		
Bombarde	16	Plein Jeu	—		
Trompette	8	Clarinette	8		
Clairon	4	Trompette	8		
		Clairon	4		

PEDALES DE COMBINAISON, 15		PEDALE 8 STOPS	
			ft.
Tirasse Grand Orgue	Anches Pédale	Quintatön	32
„ Positif		Contrebasse	16
„ Récit		Flûte	8
Grand Orgue Sur Machine	„ Grand Orgue	Octave	4
Copula Positif Sur Grand	„ Positif	Basson	16
Orgue	„ Récit.	Bombarde	16
„ Récit Sur Positif		Trompette	8
Octaves Graves Grand	Tremblant	Clairon	4
Orgue	du Récit.		
„ „ Positif			
„ „ Récit.	Expression		
	du Récit.		

It will be seen that all couplers and aids to registration are operated solely by pedal. The presence of a sub-octave coupler on each manual partly explains the French predilection for very high-pitched passages for both hands. The " Anches Pédale," etc., are ventils* silencing the reeds and Mixtures on the department in question, even though the stops are drawn. The " Grand Orgue sur machine " is really of a similar nature, silencing the Grand Orgue altogether unless it is in operation. By drawing full organ, all couplers, and all ventils, it is thus possible to make an effective build up to the full without once raising the hands from the Grand Orgue Keyboard, or touching a swell-pedal.

In the last few years in France there has been a tendency to return to the Flute foundation of the eighteenth century. The main reed chorus is often removed from the Grand Orgue and placed on the Récit, which thus tends to conform more to the English full Swell. The Positif, whenever possible, has separate Mutations and chorus upperwork. In its best development the modern French Organ is a well-balanced compromise between the organs of Clicquot and Cavaillé-Coll. Heavy-pressure voicing has made little or no headway in France. Stop control increasingly follows the English system.

(7) The Nineteenth-Century German Organ

An indescribably dreary and stodgy affair, of hardly any interest or artistic importance. Its most successful exponents were the firms of Sauer, Reubke, and Walcker.

---

* *A ventil* is a valve (operated by a drawstop or pedal) which cuts off the wind supply from the wind-chest it affects. Unless it be open, no pipes on that wind-chest will, therefore, be able to sound, even though the stops be drawn.

(8) The Early English Organ

Although the British organ prior to about 1840 was of such arrested development, it apparently satisfied many generations of musicians from Tallis onwards, including such names as Byrd, Bull, Gibbons, Purcell, Arne, Boyce and many others. Its development, especially from the mid-nineteenth-century onwards, will be more appropriately discussed in chapter III.

(9) The " Baroque Revival "

It may not be out of place to say a few words about the so-called " Baroque Revival," which, although it has hardly touched this country, has made remarkable progress in France, Germany, and America since about 1925. It may be said to have two manifestations. In its more extreme form, which is mostly found in Germany, it consists of a somewhat slavish copy of the seventeenth and eighteenth-century organs. Perhaps the most successful and least slavish example is that built in 1937 by the Aeolian Skinner Company, in the Germanic Museum, Harvard University, U.S.A. A series of paid-admission Bach recitals on this instrument resulted in all tickets being sold on every occasion. Not only organ-lovers, but the general musical public came, and the musical critics gave unqualified praise. Even allowing that America seems more ready to fly to extremes and novelties than we are in England, the success of this venture does at least provide food for thought. The instrument is by no means large, possessing the following stops, voiced on 2½-inch wind. The action is electric, and there are no swell boxes.

HAUPTWERK 8 *Stops*		POSITIV 8 *Stops*		PEDALE, 8 *Stops and* 1 *borrowed*	
	ft.		*ft.*		*ft.*
Quintade	... 16	Koppelflöte ...	8	Bourdon ...	16
Principal	... 8	Nachthorn ...	4	Gedacktbass ...	8
Spitzflöte	... 8	Nazard ...	2⅔	Principal ...	8
Octave	... 4	Blockflöte ...	2	Nachthorn ...	4
Rohrflöte	... 4	Tierce ...	1⅗	Blockflöte ...	2
Quint ...	... 2⅔	Sifflöte ...	1	Fourniture ...	IV
Superoctave	... 2	Cymbel ...	III	Posaune ⎱ Ex-	16
Fourniture	... IV	Krummhorn	8	Trompet ⎰ tended	8
				Krummhorn	
				(from Positiv)	4

The contrast between Hauptwerk and Positiv is mainly of quality, the difference in power not being very marked. The Positiv is all flutey in quality, except the Cymbel, which is of diapason tone and, of course, the Krummhorn. In its less extreme form, the Baroque Revival organ is an instrument which its adherents claim shall be equally fitted for the performance of both ancient and modern organ music. One of the best designs is that of the Aeolian Skinner instrument, at Groton, U.S.A., constructed in 1935. The specification is as follows :—

PEDALE 5-in. Wind, 16 Stops and 4 borrowed Unenclosed		GREAT ORGAN 3-in. Wind, 15 Stops Unenclosed		SWELL ORGAN $3\frac{3}{4}$-in. Wind, 18 Stops Enclosed	
	ft.		ft.		ft.
Contrabass ...	32	Subprincipal .	16	Flûte Conique ...	16
Principal ...	16	Principal ...	8	Geigen	8
Bourdon ...	16	Diapason ...	8	Gedeckt ...	8
Flûte Conique (Swell) ...	16	Harmonic Flute	8	Viole de Gambe	8
		Gemshorn ...	8	Viole Céleste ...	8
Contrabass (extended) ...	16	Grossquint ...	$5\frac{1}{3}$	Echo Viole ...	8
Grossquint ...	$10\frac{2}{3}$	Octave ...	4	Geigen	4
Octave ...	8	Principal ...	4	Flûte Triangu- laire	4
Flûte Ouverte	8	Grossterz ...	$3\frac{1}{5}$	Fugara	4
Gedeckt (Swell)	8	Quint ...	$2\frac{2}{3}$	Nazard	$2\frac{2}{3}$
Contrabass (extended) ...	8	Superoctave .	2	Fifteenth ...	2
Quint	$5\frac{1}{3}$	Tierce ...	$1\frac{3}{5}$	Tierce	$1\frac{3}{5}$
Superoctave ...	4	Full Mixture, 12, 15, 19, 22	IV	Plein Jeu, 12, 15, 19, 22, 26, 29 ...	VI
Harmonic Flute	4	Fourniture, 15, 19, 22, 26	IV	Voix Humaine ...	8
Gedeckt (Swell)	4	Cymbal, 29, 33, 36 ...	III	Bombarde ...	16
Mixture, 17, 19, 22 ...	III			Trompette ...	8
Fourniture 22, 26, 29 ...	III			Trompette ...	8
English Horn (Choir) ...	16			Clarion	4
Bombarde ...	16				
Trompette ...	8				
Clarion ...	4				

CHOIR ORGAN 3¾-in. Wind Enclosed, 10 Stops		POSITIV 2½-in. Wind Unenclosed, 8 Stops	
	ft.		ft.
Quintatön	16	Rohrflöte	8
Dulciana	8	Principal	4
Unda Maris	8	Koppelflöte	4
Orchestral Flute ...	8	Nazard	2⅔
Viola	8	Blockflöte	2
Lieblichflöte	4	Tierce	1⅗
Zauberflöte	2	Sifflöte	1
English Horn	16	Scharf, 19, 22, 26, 29 ...	IV
Clarinet	8		
Trompette	8		

It will be seen that large Diapasons and heavy-pressure reeds are absent. A good deal is claimed for the Groton organ. In this country, however, an organ of some 70 speaking stops would be regarded as wasteful in design, and also deficient in resources, unless it could produce Tuba effects when required. However, apart from this, the specification does seem in other respects to be that of an instrument which could provide suitable registration for a great variety of styles and periods in organ music. The following features are noteworthy: the fully developed flue choruses of Pedale, Great and Positiv; the contrast in ensembles between the fluework Great and the predominantly reedy Swell chorus; and the adequate provision of solo Mutations, modern Flutes, Strings and solo reeds except, of course, the Tuba. It appears from descriptions that the chorus reeds approximate to the French style, and it therefore seems doubtful to what extent they would find acceptance in this country, though a specimen or two could well be included for the sake of completeness and variety.

The authors must make it clear that while one of them (C. C.) has some experience of the Baroque Revival movement in France, neither of them has heard the American examples and they are, therefore, dependent on hearsay as to their effect. The schemes are included as interesting specifications, and as examples of this school of organ-building. American opinion on the subject is evidently hotly divided.

Chapter II

EARLY FORMS OF REGISTRATION

(1) Seventeenth and Eighteenth-Century German School

Anyone who understands the character and design of an instrument is well on the way towards knowing how to use it. So that, if our rather long first chapter has succeeded in conveying to the reader a fairly clear mental picture of the eighteenth-century French and German organ, its perusal will not have been an effort wasted.

Registration is, broadly speaking, of two kinds : one in which the hands are confined to the same keyboard, for ensemble playing, all the parts being of equal importance ; and the other in which the parts are contrasted, as in the Bach Trio Sonatas. Ensemble playing presents the fewest problems and it is convenient to consider it in its relationship to the performance of Bach's Fugues.

The modern method of treating them is well enough known. The subject is announced on a soft or mezzoforte 8-ft. stop and the power is built up with reeds and Mixtures to a great climax. Episodes are played with softer combinations, and changes of manual and registration are made as inconspicuous as possible by use of the swell pedal. That such a treatment is superficially attractive, few will deny, and it has the authority of long-standing tradition ; but when following it, the player should at least realise that it is quite opposed to the original idiom, having been conceived (as was Czerny's edition of the " 48 ") at a time when the Bach tradition was quite out of memory. In his masterly preface to the Oxford University Press edition of the 48 Preludes and Fugues, the late Professor Tovey wrote : " The facts nowadays ascertainable about Bach's style leave no excuse for basing ' instructive editions ' on the habits and traditions of pianists, however eminent, who have neglected or failed to ascertain those facts." And for " pianist " he would, had the context demanded it, no doubt have written " organist," with fully equal relevance.

Of Bach's registration there is, unfortunately, little contemporary evidence since Forkel, who might have told us so much, is silent. In the Schübler Chorale Trios Bach himself indicated the pitches to be used—16-ft., 8-ft., or 4-ft.; in the Orgelbüchlein he marked the number of manuals to be employed and in the Dorian Toccata he or a pupil marked the manual changes.

Despite this scarcity, there is a fair concensus of opinion between modern scholarship and ancient tradition ; and among modern scholars, none stands higher than Dr. Albert Schweitzer, both on account of his book, " J. S. Bach " (English translation by Ernest Newman, published by A. & C. Black Ltd.), and his and Widor's joint edition of Bach's organ works. The following is a contracted excerpt from his book, dealing with the respective merits of ancient and modern organs for playing Bach, and giving Schweitzer's views on the registration employed by Bach for his Preludes and Fugues. He writes : " We have lost the old tone of the organ that Bach wrote for, and since the tone is the chief thing, it must be said that the modern organ is not so suitable for Bach playing as is generally supposed. Our registers are all voiced too loudly or too softly. The lighter manuals are weak in comparison with the Great Organ ; they usually lack the necessary Mixtures. Our pedals are coarse and clumsy and also poor in Mixtures, as well as in 4-ft. stops."

Continuing on the subject of registration Schweitzer writes : " As a rule, Bach kept to the characteristic registration with which he began, getting variety and gradation in his playing by transition from one manual to another. We must keep to the principle that every Fugue and every Prelude is to begin and end on the Great Organ. It is quite wrong to give out a fugue theme ' p ' or ' pp ' and let each voice, as it enters, take it up more loudly."

On these general lines one may, therefore, feel reasonably justified in stating how he would have been likely to register the great Preludes and Fugues on the Steinkirchen instrument described in chapter I. On the Hauptwerk he would probably have used the 8-ft. and 4-ft. stops, and the 2-ft. Oktave and Mixture. On the Oberwerk he would have drawn the 8-ft. and 4-ft. stops, and the 2-ft. Oktave, Quint $2\frac{2}{3}$ ft., and Scharf. As a rule manual reeds would not be used, but some or all of the pedal reeds would generally be in action. It is recorded that Bach often drew 16-ft. manual stops in Fugue playing, though it must be remembered that such stops in a Schnitger organ do not have such a thickening effect as do such stops in modern organs.

If the climax of the work was emphasised by any change of registration it would have been by coupling or possibly by drawing the Cymbel. There is, however, some uncertainty as to whether the manual Trumpet would have been drawn as a chorus reed at any time. Schweitzer holds the view that Bach would not have been averse to drawing manual reeds with the flue chorus, and it does appear that the strict segregation of flue and reed choruses was losing ground in Germany in Bach's day. No doubt, he would have been influenced more than anything by the quality of each individual stop, and by whether or not it happened to be in tune. Schweitzer adds the warning, however, that most modern reeds are too powerful for use in this way. At Steinkirchen the manual Trumpet is entirely appropriate for chorus use, though it does not add appreciably to the full Hauptwerk. Minor refinements such as these will remain matters for conjecture, but the main framework is tolerably certain.

The Hauptwerk chorus was, indeed, fairly powerful, but not at all thick, nor so powerful as to become exhausting by prolonged use. The Pedal chorus, with its plentiful reeds, ensured clarity without over-emphasis. The brilliant chorus of the Oberwerk was contrasted in quality with that of the Hauptwerk, rather than in power. The whole instrument was specifically designed for the clear delineation of polyphonic music, and whether one likes it or not, it was pre-eminently suited for this particular purpose. It is much to be regretted that there is in England no such instrument upon which Bach can be played as he himself played and as he unquestionably meant his music to be heard.

The change on to the second manual for the lighter episodal passages was well marked, for there was no swell pedal to slur it over. It must be remembered that Bach came at the end of a period of musical tradition which had looked to sharp antiphonal contrasts for dramatic effect. The idea of a crescendo apparently never occurred to composers of that time. Certainly they had none available on the organ, but they could have had a crescendo and diminuendo in their orchestra had they so desired. Yet one has only to listen to the Brandenburg Concerti to realise that the idea of what is commonly called " expression " hardly entered Bach's mind, and we know as an historical fact that the development of the orchestral crescendo took place some years after his death. We may, therefore, safely assume that Bach would not have been greatly interested in the use of the swell pedal, at least in fugal playing. Far from wishing to camouflage it, he would certainly relish the sharp contrast between the different manual choruses.

Should the reader wish to try out a Bach Fugue with registration such as the composer might have used, he may find that his organ seems at first sight absolutely unsuited for the purpose. Yet by ingenuity, apparently unpromising material may be adapted to give approximately the desired effect. An interesting experiment in this connection was carried out, at the Church of St. Margaret, Lee, on a normal modern church organ of some 35 speaking stops, which seemed but poorly suited to the requirements of eighteenth-century registration. The Great possesses a stopped double, two Open Diapasons and is complete to Twelfth and Fifteenth with a semi-Tuba. The Swell fluework includes a Mixture and an extension family of 16-ft., 8-ft. and 4-ft. Trumpets. The enclosed Choir is of normal design and the Pedal fluework mainly consists of an Open Wood of no great definition. It also possesses a powerful Trombone, but its great asset from a Bach registration point of view is that the Swell Trumpet unit is also available on the Pedals in 16-ft., 8-ft. and 4-ft. pitches.

For Bach playing, the Great Organ large Diapason was far too ponderous in tone, so only the small one was used, being a little softer than the Principal. To these were added the Twelfth, Fifteenth, and Swell Diapason chorus coupled in unison and octave pitch. On the pedals were drawn the

16-ft., 8-ft. and 4-ft. Swell reeds, the Bourdon 16-ft. and Octave Wood 8-ft. Complete Preludes were played on this registration, the episodes being performed on the Swell flue-work. Compared with a normal modern treatment, one could not fail to be struck by the exceptional clarity resulting from the exclusion of all Flute and reed tone, and powerful 8-ft. stops from the manuals. The unusual provision of mezzoforte pedal reeds in 16-ft., 8-ft. and 4-ft. pitches also enabled one to appreciate the remarkable value of such stops in preserving a clear-cut pedal outline.

One school of thought might suggest that such a treatment became monotonous, but there could be no question that it enabled the architectural nobility of the works to be better appreciated. In any case, the experiment is well worth trying, as it will give a better idea of Bach's own ensemble playing than pages of print will convey. That no other form of treatment was even possible on an eighteenth-century organ is shown by the following passage from a very remark-able French book published in 1921 entitled " L'Esthétique de l'Orgue," by Jean Huré. It is written with a wealth of Gallic enthusiasm, and the following is a somewhat condensed paraphrase of the passage in question :—

" I had been invited abroad to give a series of recitals on some very ancient organs. ' Some very old organs.' To me that implied instruments in poor condition with four-octave manuals and a short compass Récit. Well, I found myself confronted by a three-manual organ* with an army of stops, innocent of composition pedals, swell boxes, couplers, or other aids to registration. I examined the list of stops—

---

* Unfortunately, the author does not disclose the identity of this remarkable instrument, but from his description of it, a Netherlands design seems to be suggested.

sixty of them. There were only three manual reeds (Voix Humaine, Cromorne, and Trompette) and two on the pedals (Trompette 8 and Clairon 4) ; only one 16-ft. stop on the pedals (an open Flute), although both Grand Orgue and Positif each had an open Montre 16-ft. of very soft intonation. On each of these departments were three 8-ft. stops and, by contrast, three 4-ft. on the Grand Orgue, and four each on Positif, Récit, and Pédale. There were altogether eight 2-ft. stops in the organ and two 1-ft. All the other stops were Mutations—a Fourniture, at least, on each clavier, a Cymbale on the Grand Orgue and a Carillon on the Positif. Cornets of 16-ft. and 8-ft. pitch, Tierces of $3\frac{1}{5}$ and $1\frac{3}{5}$ ft., Quintes, Nazards, Larigots and a Sesquialtera completed the picture. The Pédale possessed Quints of $10\frac{2}{3}$ and $5\frac{1}{3}$ ft. and a Cornet of 4-ft. pitch.

" I was absolutely aghast—how could I possibly play Bach on an instrument which, to my ignorant mind, seemed completely impracticable ?

" I had learnt to register Bach on the usual French formula—full on each Clavier for the fortes, some echoes on Récit and Positif ; sometimes the 8-ft. fluework with occasional 4-ft. additions—and that was all. I had always found it rather boring and monotonous, but I had resigned myself to it from childhood, timidly reflecting (without liking to voice my feelings) that the works of Bach read better than they played. When our teachers played them I was like everyone else—politely bored.

" Yet, when I read them, I mentally pictured beautiful ringing tone-qualities, gay and clear, like the colours of gothic stained glass windows.

" I observed that the organ upon which I was condemned,

some hours later, to give my opening recital, was in fine condition. Each flue stop was perfectly tuned and regulated, but so soft as to seem almost feeble ; yet the tone was full, and carried well. The reeds had little éclat, and their timbre seemed a little dry, almost reminiscent of free-reed stops. But their attack was amazing ; it seemed almost percussive.

This was all very well, but what could one do with this string of Mutations ? I had always learnt that Mixtures were weapons of power, to be brought on only with the reeds. In desperation, I pulled out everything except the Voix Humaine and started on the D Minor Toccata.

" What a feast of sound it was ! The magical richness of the voices was like a sort of musical miracle. I heard an infinity of joyous luminous voices. Every detail was brought out with an incisive precision that I had never heard before ; each voice was absolutely distinct. The lighter episodes, played on Récit or Positif, seemed to come from two other organs, while each manual had its own individual character. One sparkled with octaves and high-pitched quints ; another was endowed with a more sombre quality by virtue of its Cornets and tierces. The sole 16-ft. pedal stop (a Grosse Flöte, very soft, yet distinct) seemed somehow deeper than the 32-ft. at Nôtre Dame or St. Sulpice, but in place of that leaden heaviness peculiar to our modern organs, the sonority here was clear and ringing.

" The splendid effect of the Bach Toccata brought to life in a flash what I had been picturing mentally, and what neither my friends nor I had been able to realise in fact. This organ, built in the time of the old masters, and piously preserved without alteration, at once showed me the composer's intentions, and I could not choose but to obey.

" The Toccata finished, I began to wonder about the registration of the fugue. I suppressed only the reeds, and played the subject on the Positif, from which I also withdrew a Cornet and Carillon that seemed too brilliant, leaving a Fourniture and some Quints. The episodes I played on the Récit until the re-entry of the pedals, after which I transferred to the Grand Orgue, where Flute tone predominated ; then echos on different manuals, during which I again drew the Positif Cornet, and finally, before the closing climax, when the chords can be played with one hand, I drew successively the reeds and Carillon, ending with a most joyful sound. In an instant I had, by a chance meeting with this instrument learnt much more than during years of study. Next, I tried the D Major Fugue, and found that on such an organ there was nothing monotonous about it, although played without change of stops or manuals, except at the end, when I added the pedal reeds, whose attack was as incisive as a harpsichord. Nowadays, it is not advisable to play very rapid passages on reed stops, but this was not the advice of the ancients, as is proved by the numerous rapid passages in their solos for Trompette and Cromorne.

" Thus it was that some old organ forced me to discover, if not how to play, at least how to register the works of Bach. It was through no merit of mine, but on such an instrument, one could hardly do otherwise."

*   *   *   *

This detailed record of a remarkable musical experience by a prominent musician is surely more instructive and convincing than a host of researches and detailed examples. Huré afterwards discovered that Guilmant and Saint-Saens were already advocating the registration of Bach on the lines which he had thus worked out empirically for himself.

By comparison, it is quaint to recall a conversation which took place between a friend of the authors and a sound professional musician trained by a well-known cathedral organist. "Have you," he asked the organist, "studied the history of the organ?" To a reply in the affirmative he then asked, "Don't you think the modern organ is a bad instrument for the playing of Bach?" "Oh, yes," answered the organist, "*it's all those mixtures and things*"!

By this time, the reader will have grasped the fundamental difference which exists between modern and eighteenth-century registration. In the modern organ, we have so many varieties of tone in 8-ft. pitch that we *apparently* need to look no further for the registration of such contrasted solos, duos, and trios as we may require. Apart from the Diapason choruses, very few modern instruments possess solo or accompanimental registers in other than 8-ft. and 4-ft. pitches. But up to the end of the eighteenth-century this was not so, and the organist got his variety by combining stops of different pitches. The complete modern organ, possessing both solo voices and solo Mutations, may intermingle the two, combining a modern String stop, for example, with solo Mutations, or counterfeiting a Vox Humana with a Dulciana, Nazard, Tierce and Tremolo.

At this juncture the reader might logically exclaim: "Why should I bother with these synthetic effects when the skill of the modern voicer provides me with the real thing?" The eminent composer and organist Mr. Guy Weitz, who is equally at home with every style and period of organ music, has made an instructive commentary on this point, when writing in the "Rotunda" in 1929.

"It has been said, and quite truly, that the Tierce and

Nazard, together with the Viole 8-ft., produce a new timbre closely resembling the orchestral oboe; that the same mutation stops associated with the 8-ft. Flute give the impression of a clarinet, and so on; but it is time to point out that these new timbres remain essentially real organ tones which nothing else could replace. I am sure that I admire unreservedly the Clarinet, the Cor Anglais and other modern stops which have been brought to perfection; but I would every time give preference to the Nazard and Tierce in a small scale or moderate size organ, were I forced to choose one or the other. And this for the good reason that the Clarinet, the Orchestral Oboe and other solo stops can be used only as such; their individuality being too pronounced, they cannot take their place in an ensemble. On the other hand, the Nazard and the Tierce, not to mention the other Mutations, lend themselves to a great number of most effective combinations for solo playing, and also they blend exceedingly well with Diapason and reed choruses."

When early composers are scant in their marks of registration, one can reconstruct what they did only by literary research, and experiment on such early organs as remain in original condition. In this, Mr. Weitz is one of the authorities who can be relied upon with confidence, and in the same article in the "Rotunda" he comments interestingly upon the following well-known Bach examples.

"Let us take a chorale of Bach, for instance, No. 51, 'Wenn Wir in Hochsten Nothen Sein.' The parts of the left hand and pedal are easy enough, but what stops shall we choose for the solo part? An 8-ft. Flute might be too dull, an Oboe too distant; a Diapason would not have the required flexibility. But if to a Flute 8-ft. or Cor de Nuit we add a 4-ft. Flute and Nazard we shall find that this combination gives us a timbre of exquisite freshness, a genuine organ tone which no other single stop could produce. For the treble melody in the Chorale ' Ich ruf' zu dir, Herr Jesu Christ ' from the Orgelbüchlein, the most suitable combination would be the Nazard and Tierce with a Flute 8-ft. or Viole 8-ft. The Nazard with the Flutes 8-ft. and 4-ft. will again produce a most delightful effect in such pieces as the Andante of the third Trio Sonata by Bach. As to the finale of the same work, could one wish anything better than Cor de Nuit 8-ft., Flute 4-ft., Nazard 2⅔-ft. for the right hand, Bassoon or Oboe 8-ft. and Flute 8-ft. for the left hand."

Nevertheless, if Bach left only scant directions on his compositions, he did give us one valuable document which shows something at first hand of his ideas about registration. This is contained in his recommendations to the Muhlhausen Council for the rebuilding of the organ in the Church of Blaise in that town. Among other things, he demanded a 32-ft. Sub-Bass to give a proper foundation of tone. He evidently felt that the Pedal Organs of his day were lacking in depth and dignity of tone, because, in another report, on the Leipzig Johanneskirche instrument, we find him complaining that the Pedal Trombone and Trumpet were inclined to speak roughly instead of with pure steady tone.

At Muhlhausen, he asked that the 8-ft. Trumpet on the upper manual should be replaced by a 16-ft. Fagotto, " whose introduction will permit many new combinations of tone and the more delicate accompaniment of figural music." The Gemshorn on the same manual was to be replaced by an 8-ft. Viola da Gamba, " which will blend admirably with the 4-ft. Salicional on the Ruckpositiv." The 2⅔-ft. chorus Quint was to be replaced by a 2⅔-ft. solo Nazard.

Most interesting—a whole new Brustwerk department was specified. Various interpretations have been put upon " three principalia," but the following translation is taken from that great work " J. S. Bach, A Biography," by the late Charles Sanford Terry :—

" Three Principals in the front, namely, a 2⅔-ft. Quint, a 2-ft. Octave and an 8-ft. Schalmei, all of good tin.
A Mixture r ranks.
A Tertia, which, in combination with other stops, gives a fine sesquialtera tone.
A soft 4-ft. Flute and, lastly :
An 8-ft. Stillgedeckt to fill out the continuo, when accompanying figural music. If made of wood it will be more resonant than a metal Gedeckt."
(A Stillgedeckt approximates to an early English Stopped Diapason.)

All this was duly carried out, and when he opened the rebuilt organ in 1709, Bach is reported to have played the Choral Prelude " Ein' Feste Burg," in which he registered the new 16-ft. Fagotto on the upper manual for the left hand, and his " Sesquialtera tone " on the Brustwerk, for the right.

*   *   *   *

The Cornet has already been mentioned. In the original form it generally consisted of a Chimney Flute 8 ft. and lightly-blown open metal ranks of 4-ft., 2⅔-ft., 2-ft. and 1⅗-ft. pitches, all of large scale. A Cornet might also be made up of independent stops in these pitches, to which could be added the 19th or Larigot, imparting a more ringing quality of tone. (The 19th is the most powerful harmonic of a Trumpet.) Mr. Weitz remarks that the piquancy of a Cornet will serve to brighten up many passages which might otherwise be dull. This certainly applies to much of the music of the eighteenth-century English composer John Stanley, who wrote many florid passages which are very tedious when played on anything with less colour. Yet, properly registered, much of his very simple music has quite a charm which deserves better than the almost complete oblivion commonly accorded to it. It is a great loss that the old Cornets were so ruthlessly weeded out from our organs in the nineteenth-century, and their re-introduction by the more advanced modern builders is a matter for congratulation.

Much valuable research on the registration of early music on Schnitger and similar organs has been carried out by Straube and Ramin, and their findings are made available in one of the Peters editions of " Old Masters." To anyone possessing this important work, it is the best guide one could have, but for the benefit of those not so fortunate, the following examples will suffice to give a clear insight into the handling of a Schnitger organ. Some of the recommendations may appear quite absurd, but if one remembers the tonal characteristics of the Schnitger organ, as described in Chapter I, it should become fairly easy to judge how they would sound. The following abbreviations are used : Hw—Hauptwerk, Ow—Oberwerk, Rp—Ruckpositiv, Bw—Brustwerk.

(a) *Sweelinck* (1610). Variations on " My young life hath an end " :—

Theme and 1st variation, *p*. Rp : Blockflöte 4, Gedackt 8.

2nd variation, *mp*. Ow : Holzflöte 8, Gemshorn 2.

3rd variation, *mf*. Rp : Quintatön 8, Octave 4, Sifflöte 2, Sesquialtera 2 rk.

4th variation, *f*. Bw : Trechter Regal 8, Waldflöte 2, Sesquialtera 2 rks.

5th variation, *f*. Hw : Quintatön 16, Oktave 8, Mixture.

6th variation, *mp*. Rp : Quintatön 8, Oktave 4, Sifflöte 1⅓, Sesquialtera 2 rks.

(b) *Schlick* (1512). Choral : " Maria zart von edler Art." Hw : Rohrflöte 4 ; Ow : Trompete 4 ; Ped : Oktave 8.

(c) *Buxtehude* (1700). Choralvorspiel : " Lobt Gott, ihr Christen, allzugleich." Hw : Rohrflöte 4 ; Ow : Spitzflöte 4, Nasat 2⅔, Tremolo ; Ped : Oktave 8.

(d) *Frescobaldi* (c. 1610). Canzona. Hw : Oktave 8, Oktave 4 ; Ped : Oktave 16, Oktave 4.

(e) *Pachelbel* (c. 1700). Toccata. Hw : Rohrflöte 4 ; Mixture ; Ow : Oktave 4, Oktave 2, Gemshorn 2, Cymbel, 3 ranks. Ped : Oktave 2, Nachthorn 2.

(f) *Pachelbel.* Choralvorspiel : " Durch Adams Fall ist ganz verderbt." Hw : Oktave 2, Mixture ; Rp : Dulcian 16, Nasat 2⅔, Oktave 2, Sesquialtera 2 ranks.

(g) *Daquin* (c. 1750). " Noel." Fonds Flûtes 8 and 4-ft., with solos on Hautbois and Cornet.

(h) *Praetorius* (c. 1600). Hymnus : " O Lux Beata Trinitus " (manual canon with theme in the pedals). Hw : Rohrflöte 4 ; Ow : Spitzflöte 4 ; Ped : Trompete 4.

(i) *Scheidt* (1624). Fuga Contraria. Hw : Quintatön 16 ; Ow : Vox Humana 8 ; Rp : Quintatön ; Ped : Oktave 16.

(j) *Scheidt* (1624). Fuga Contraria :

Hw :	Ow :	Rp :	Ped :
ft.	*ft.*	*ft.*	*ft.*
Quintatön 16	Vox Humana 8	Quintatön 8	Oktave 16
Oktave 8	Spitzflöte 4	Oktave 2	Oktave 8
Rohrflöte 4	Nasat 2⅔	Sesquialtera	Oktave 2
Mixture	Gemshorn 2	2 ranks	Mixture

(k) *Scheidt.* Sacred Song (Theme and Variations) : " Warum betrubst du dich, mein Hertz " :

ft.		*ft.*		*ft.*
Hw : Rohrflöte 4	Ow : Holzflöte 8		Gemshorn 2	
Rp : Quintatön 8	Blockflöte	4	Bw : Dulcian 8	
Waldflöte 2	Ped : Nachthorn 2			

(*l*) *Titelouze* (*c.* 1600). "Pange Lingua Gloriosi" (Theme in Pedals ; Contrapuntal working in manuals ; 3 variations). Soft unisons and Mixtures on each manual. Ped : Soft 4-ft. reed only.

(*m*) *Froberger* (*c.* 1660). Ricercare.

Hw :		Ow :		Rp :		Ped :	
	ft.		ft.		ft.		ft.
Oktave	8	Rohrflöte	8	Gedackt	8	Subass	16
Oktave	4	Trompete	4	Blockflöte	4	Couplers	
Flachflöte	2	Nasat	2⅔				
		Gemshorn	2				

Commenting briefly on these, it is seen that more than one 8-ft. stop is never drawn on any manual ; the effects are obtained solely by the combination of stops of different pitches. How self-sufficient were the Mixtures is shown by such markings as " Rohrflöte 4-ft. and Mixture." The actual Mixture so frequently called for by Straube and Ramin was one composed entirely of quints and unisons, possessing six ranks in the bass, increasing to 8 ranks in the treble. The small, buzzing tone of the Schnarrwerk stops has been mentioned. This would be in large measure covered up by the higher-pitched Mutations with which they were used, so that only a slight reed characteristic would be apparent—provided they were in tune. Such combinations as Trechter Regal 8-ft., Waldflöte 2-ft., Sesquialtera 12, 17 ; or Dulcian 16-ft., Nasat 2⅔-ft., Octave 2-ft., Sesquialtera 12, 17 ; or Dulcian 8-ft., Waldflöte 2-ft., from the examples quoted above, are cases in point. Such reed stops would be of about the same power as our modern Vox Humana, a stop, which though grossly mis-used, has far greater combinational possibilities than is generally recognised.

It is noticeable that no hesitation is felt in using a 4-ft. foundation in such soft pieces as Schlick's " Maria Zart von edler Art," and the single stop on each manual, in that example and elsewhere, is a remarkable anticipation of Parratt's plea for the more general use of single stops. This playing at 4-ft. pitch is, of course, only tolerable with very mildly voiced registers.

In many cases, a 2-ft. stop is added to an 8-ft. without any intermediate 4-ft. If one considers this, it is quite a logical proceeding : 4-ft. flue stops (except Strings) add little of brightness or colour ; they add more of power and solidity, and that is how the Germans mainly considered them. So, if they merely wanted colouring matter, they drew a 2-ft. stop or Sesquialtera, and left the 4-ft. out. The same also applies to the pedals. An open 8-ft. register will add much drive and power to the 16-ft. stops ; but if definition alone is required, a 4-ft. stop will more adequately meet the case.

A further word may, perhaps, be said about the practicability of employing an historically correct form of registration on an English organ, the question of ensemble playing having already been touched upon. On instruments where the only upperwork consists of powerful Diapasons the thing is clearly impossible, but on properly designed organs with solo Mutations it is relatively easy. The extension organ, in particular, affords many possibilities, and whatever the merits or demerits that this system may possess, it does unquestionably open out great vistas of registration by combining stops of different pitches ; this point will be further enlarged upon in Chapter IV. Again, on many organs made before the last quarter of the nineteenth-century (and on Willis organs until the turn of the century) the Diapason upperwork, although there are no specific solo Mutations, is yet sufficiently mild to be used in that capacity. A number of old Mixtures containing a tierce are found to break at middle C to 12, 15, 17, so that one only has to combine such a stop with 8-ft. and 4-ft. Flutes to have a solo melodic Cornet. Indeed, when such Mixtures are of flutey tone, they are better adapted to serve as solo Mutations rather than as chorus Mixtures. Other possibilities are Flutes 8-ft. and 4-ft. and Twelfth ; Swell Gedeckt and Mixture ; Swell Oboe and Fifteenth ; Choir Dulciana and Piccolo, or Clarinet and Piccolo, and so on. For small Brustwerk choruses, the Swell Gedeckt, Principal, Fifteenth and Mixture with box open, is almost invariably a successful effect.

Before leaving German registration, a few words may be said about the playing of Handel, whose organ compositions were restricted by the small, English organs of his day, without pedals. He, therefore, confined himself to a fairly light and sparkling style of writing. Some of his organ compositions, like his choruses, do indeed lend themselves to a bolder treatment ; but, generally, the use of powerful reeds and even the more powerful Diapasons in his music is inartistic, and the crashing climaxes indulged in by many organists are a cheap form of playing to the gallery. When playing with a big modern orchestra, the organist naturally has no alternative but to bring his heavy guns into action.

Some music is so lofty in style that it depends but little on the medium used. This more particularly applies to Bach, and it explains why his music is impressive when registered in a style so foreign to that which he himself employed. But with lesser and earlier composers, and even in the case of Buxtehude, this does not apply. If they are not played in the right atmosphere, they become almost incomprehensible, and their splendid music is so widely ignored, mainly because so few people have any idea of how it ought to sound.

(2) Seventeenth and Eighteenth-Century French Organ Registration

This reliance on historically suitable registration applies even more strongly to the highly formal—almost artificial—style of the early French composers. The effect is absolutely dependent upon registration closely following that specified, and the composers were far more lavish in their marks of registration than were their German contemporaries. In the main, they relied upon a fairly small number of standardised combinations, and we also have plenty of documentary evidence, especially in Dom Bédos' " L'art du facteur d'orgues " already mentioned.

Although much of this music is amazingly thin, on a suitable organ its effect can be majestic, gay, or sombre according to the mood of the composer. It is essential, however, that it should be registered more or less as directed.

The whole of Dom Bédos' directions could advantageously be quoted here, but the following paraphrased excerpts cover the more important and usual contingencies. If read in conjunction with the 1675 specification given in Chapter I, and the earlier remarks about its flue and reed choruses, a good idea should be formed of the effects which the composers had in mind.

Plein Jeu. All the Montres and open 8-ft. stops, all Bourdons, Prestants, Doublettes, Fournitures, both on the Grand Orgue and Positif. The manuals may be coupled. On the Pédale, all the reeds, but *no* flue stops. The Plein Jeu should be treated " with grave and majestic movements ; with great flights of harmony, interwoven with the art of syncopation, striking discords, suspensions and new harmonic devices. The Plein Jeu on the Positif needs clear playing."

Grand Jeu. The Cornet, Prestant, and all the Trompettes and Clairons of the Grand Orgue, and Positif, coupled. Pédale as for the Plein Jeu.

Grand Jeu de Tierce. Foundation stops from 32-ft. up to Nazard, Tierce, and Quarte de Nazard 2-ft., but *not* the Doublette 2-ft. (This belongs to the chorus ensemble, while the Quarte belongs to the Mutation series, being, as its name implies, a fourth above the Nazard.)

For a slow and grave Fugue. On the Grand Orgue, Prestant, all Trompettes, and Clairons. On the Positif, Trompette, Clairon and Cromorne. Positif coupled to Grand Orgue. Pédale, Trompettes and Clairons. (This seems very remarkable when compared with the German system, but it must be remembered that Dom Bédos' idea of a Fugue was not the same as Bach's. For the latter's " great flights of harmony, striking discords and suspensions," Bédos would have had no hesitation in specifying the Plein Jeu.)

Tierce en Taille. (*a*) Accompaniment on two or three 8-ft. stops on the Grand Orgue and Pédale flue-work. (*b*) Solo in the tenor, to be " ornamented with taste," on two 8-ft., Flute 4-ft., Nazard 2⅔-ft., Quarte de Nazard 2-ft., Tierce 1⅗-ft., and Larigot 1⅓-ft.

Solo Trompette. The same accompaniment will serve.

Basse de Trompette. Grand Orgue : Prestant, Trompettes, and Clairons. Positif : two 8-ft., Doublette 2-ft., Larigot 1⅓-ft.

Récits de dessus (*i.e.,* high-pitched solos). Accompany on two 8-ft. stops. Suitable solos are Cromorne and Prestant ; Trompette de Récit ; Cornet du Récit ; Jeu de Tierce du Positif.

Solo on the Voix Humaine. To the Voix Humaine add Bourdon 8-ft., Flute 4-ft., and perhaps a Prestant 4-ft. or Nazard 2⅔-ft. The Tremulant may be used if it is a good one. (Most English Tremulants, incidentally, beat far too quickly, serving only to achieve a restless fluttering effect. Dom Bédos repeatedly warns players against excessive use of the

Tremulant, which he apostrophises as "le perturbateur des jeux d'orgue.")

For a " Duo " (*i.e.*, pieces in two contrasted parts) :

(a) The Grand Jeu de Tierce du Grand Orgue and the same on the Positif.

(b) Right hand : Cornet du Récit. Left hand : Prestant and Cromorne.

(c) Right hand : Cornet du Récit. Left hand : Trompette du Positif.

(d) Right hand : Trompette du Récit. Left hand : Jeu de Tierce du Positif.

For a trio on two Claviers and Pedals :

(a) (i) Cornet du Récit, (ii) Cromorne and Prestant Positif, (iii) Jeu de Tierce Pédale. Do not allow more than one octave interval between bass and treble parts.

(b) (i) Cornet du Récit, (ii) Jeu de Tierce du Positif, (iii) Pédale Flûtes, 16-ft., 8-ft. and 4-ft.

(c) (i) Trompette 8-ft., (ii) Positif 8-ft., Flûte 4-ft., Nazard 2⅔-ft., (iii) Pédale Flûtes 16-ft., 8-ft. and 4-ft.

(d) (i) Jeu de Tierce du Positif, (ii) two flue 8-ft., Grand Orgue, (iii) Pédale Flûtes 16-ft., 8-ft. and 4-ft.

To accompany a choir of voices or to play plainsong melodies. With a large choir use the Plein Jeu and a pedal bass of Trompettes and Clairons. The voices should always be predominant, and the accompaniment should serve only to sustain and embellish.

To play a plainsong melody, play the theme solemnly on the pedal reeds, to which may be added the pedal Bombarde 16-ft., where there is one. Accompany on the Plein Jeux on the Grand Orgue and Positif coupled.

Use of the Bombardes. As above, for plainsong melodies. A 16-ft. Bombarde may also be coupled to the Grand Orgue and Positif for slow and majestic effects, suspensions and final climaxes.

More or less untouched examples of eighteenth-century French organs may be found in different parts of the country, while in Paris is to be found the historic five-manual instrument at St. Gervais, upon which successive generations of the Couperin family played for some two centuries. This also is practically untouched. The Clicquot organ at St. Merry has been conservatively rebuilt. In the Versailles Palace Chapel is a modern four-manual organ (by Gonzalez) constructed entirely upon the eighteenth-century principles. On any of these, Dom Bédos' registration may be judged at first hand ; a most valuable and interesting experience.

PART 2

Chapter III

THE TONAL STRUCTURE OF THE MODERN BRITISH ORGAN

Perhaps the most engrossing subject for the players of the organ is its tonal structure. Whether regarded from the scientific or artistic point of view, its study is equally fascinating. In fact, the building up of each department by the selection of individual registers (or tone families) to form a complete and characteristic whole, in contrast with other departments, is one of the most vital questions in organ design. While first-class voicing and regularity of finish are essential in individual stops, the *methods* of voicing, important though they be, are a secondary consideration. If the design and its harmonic scheme be faulty or incomplete, the most artistic voicing cannot make good the deficiencies of its tonal structure.

Up to rather more than one hundred years ago, the English organ was in a sorry state, so far as tonal design was concerned, in comparison with its continental contemporaries. Though the Great and Choir compass often extended down to 10⅔-ft. G., and occasionally to 16-ft. C., the lower octaves were generally incomplete. The Swell compass was short, extending to middle C, or fiddle G, and sometimes to tenor C. The Pedal was still more deficient. The Pedal keys often merely depressed the corresponding notes on the manuals and occasionally controlled an incomplete set of very large-scaled open wood pipes, mis-called " Diapason," which Thomas Casson aptly termed " a huge Clarabella." From this it will be gathered that it was impossible to render Bach's organ works on English organs of that period.

In the early part of the nineteenth-century we find Greats with Mutations, compound stops and a Trumpet, but no doubles ; and Choir Organs with no doubles or chorus except a bare Fifteenth and an un-usable Clarinet. The short-compass Swell had some flue chorus, one or two 8-ft. reeds, occasionally a Clarion, and, very occasionally, a 16-ft. stop called " Double Diapason," but really a Bourdon. The poverty stricken pedal has already been noted. Within the last hundred years, however, the progress in England of organ building generally, and tonal structure in particular, has been without parallel in any other country. It is proposed to indicate how the tonal designs of the different departments have developed. A few complete schemes of instruments historically interesting will also be included.

The Great Organ

It is almost universally admitted that the Great is in every way the most important division of the organ, the success or failure of any instrument being determined by it. So far as the English organ is concerned, its tonal structure is avowedly built up on the Open Diapason in its various pitches. The Diapason tone quality has always been the unique and special glory of the organ, distinguishing it absolutely from any other instrument. The true English examples display a quality full and dignified, but comparatively deficient in harmonic upper partial tones. For this reason, though the

Open Diapason, by itself, can be tolerated for a longer period than any other organ register, it becomes, after a time, unsatisfactory to an ear familiar with the complex tonality of other instruments. We have seen that the earlier builders regarded their instrument as one huge compound stop, giving the unison rank no more prominence or importance than any other. On the other hand, it was found that unison ranks, however massed, produced tones of an ineffective character. Consequently, the introduction of octave, fifth and even third-sounding ranks was accepted as a matter of course. Their method was originally entirely empirical, but they nevertheless anticipated the scientific teaching of Helmholtz, as set forth in his classic work " The Sensations of Tone "—in 1867.

The merits of the early organs naturally varied ; but we often find high-pitched Mutations and compound stops voiced unscientifically and undesirably loud, together with thin, harsh, uneven-toned reeds. These combined to produce an effect which has been facetiously termed " sausage-frying." As will be seen later, this caused a violent reaction against flue chorus-work, which resulted in its being whittled down or omitted altogether, to the great detriment of the musical resources of the organ. Judging by the number of incomplete tonal designs one comes across at the present time, it seems doubtful whether its force has yet been entirely spent.

With these exceptions, ample flue chorus work, comprising both single and compound stops, has generally been a feature in the tonal structure of every instrument making any pretence at completeness ; at any rate, during the present century. So far as continental organs were concerned, the greatest reformer was Aristide Cavaillé-Coll, who, instead of working empirically, brought scientific reasoning to bear on the question of tone building. Not only did he demonstrate practically the importance of the complete harmonic series in the flue work, but, by his artistic perception and technical skill, he also brought the older type of open reed to a pitch of finish and perfection never before attained. Though he laid less stress than some of his predecessors on separate Mutation ranks, he provided adequate amounts of scientifically designed compound stops which included not only the tierce, but sometimes even the septième, thus completing the harmonic series in a remarkable fashion. The latter rank had already appeared in one or two English instruments under the name of " Sharp Twentieth."

The Great ensemble in this country, however, remained in the unsatisfactory state previously spoken of until about the second half of the last century, when Henry Willis came on the scene. Born in 1821, he eventually did for the English organ what Cavaillé-Coll had already accomplished in France. It is not impossible that he was influenced in more ways than one by his great French contemporary. On the one hand, he maintained a reasonable proportion of artistically voiced compound stops ; on the other, he reaped the benefit of William Hill's introduction of heavy wind for solo reed stops some fifteen years earlier—an important advance, the significance of which had not been realised, even by its inventor. Together with his brother George, he began the development of a whole series of chorus reeds voiced on heavier wind, with increased pressures in the upper part of the compass. The latter idea undoubtedly came from Cavaillé-Coll, but the Willis's employed closed shallots. By their methods of voicing, a purity and brilliance, combined with refinement and evenness of tone, and a proper balance between treble and bass never before dreamt of, was produced. We shall see later how these methods were further developed by Henry's gifted son Vincent. By their combined efforts, Willis reed voicing became a household word and enabled Henry Willis to out-distance his rivals right up to the end of his life. To the further developments of their methods, we owe all the best characteristics of present-day reed voicing.

As far back as 1855, Willis reed work was exhibited on a grand scale at St. George's Hall, Liverpool, and in tonal effect this splendid instrument could hold its own against even its most modern successors.* It is really no exaggeration to say that the renaissance of English organ-building, which began about the middle of last century, owes more to Willis than to anyone else.

Though, in the first instance, he placed heavy pressure chorus reed on the Great Organ only, it will be seen later that his work in the other departments was even more important. The striking grandeur of the Willis full Great was not questioned, but many critics had doubtless become accustomed to the thin-toned reeds of the older organs, and disregarded its beauty. They complained that the reeds were too prominent in relation to the flue stops. Some even went so far as to condemn Willis's work altogether, and to try to back up the unprogressive type. In contrast with Willis, most of the English organ-builders concentrated their efforts almost entirely on Diapasons and Flutes, leaving the Mixtures and reeds to take care of themselves ; often with disastrous results. Others omitted Mutations and compound stops altogether.

* Unfortunately, this historic hall and organ were damaged during the war by enemy action.

Towards the end of last century, attempts were made by one school, led by Robert Hope Jones, to build up a Great Organ ensemble by means of ponderous Diapasons, big Flutes, and smooth-toned Tubas. As Mixtures were to them anathema, the upperwork was restricted to a feeble Principal and a Piccolo. To supply the wanting harmonics they relied on Quintatöns and ultra-keen string-toned stops, helped out by octave couplers. In spite of the advocacy of a certain number of adherents, it was soon recognised that no real progress could be made in this direction, though it seems doubtful whether such unscientific methods of tone building are even yet quite extinct.

To play Bach or other classical organ music on such instruments would be well-nigh impossible. Attempts like these were, therefore, doomed to failure, because attention was focussed on the unison pitch to the neglect of the essential harmonic structure. As Vincent Willis once truly said : " Your principal Open Diapason must be of such a quality and power that it can, with suitable modifications, be used throughout the various intervals in the harmonic series. Unduly large 8-ft. Diapasons would be more appropriate on a third or fourth manual than on the Great."

To find a fitting counterpoise on the Great to the full-toned chorus reeds of Willis, we must look back to the tonal schemes of his other celebrated contemporary, Edmund Schulze. The Great Organ designs of the latter, in this country at any rate, were characterised by the boldness of their Diapasons generally, and of the chorus work in particular. Willis's fluework, finely proportioned though it was, never came within measurable distance of Schulze in this respect. Schulze's reed stops had most of the unsatisfactory qualities of the older type, but it mattered little, as they were quite put in the shade by the overwhelming grandeur of the flue chorus. Nevertheless, the tone quality of Schulze's full Greats was decidedly improved when the reeds were shut in. It was unfortunate that he never profited by what Willis had accomplished, though it would seem that the example had not been entirely ignored, for we find six-inch wind proposed for the Great and Pedal reeds in a design for the projected organ at Cologne Cathedral. It was equally unfortunate that Willis could never see any virtue in Schulze fluework ; otherwise (except Tewkesbury, 1885), we should not have had to wait until the present century before we find the essentials of the tonal structures of *both* masters combined in *one* instrument, though in different departments.

Well-known examples of Schulze's work exist at Doncaster, Armley, Tyne Dock, and Hindley. All have splendidly developed flue choruses, particularly Doncaster, where the Great contains three compound stops (including a Cornet) comprising no fewer than fourteen ranks of chorus. The five-rank Mixture at Armley, which, when added, appears at least to double the power of the Great, is well known. Best, after trying this organ, said : " You draw a stop labelled ' Mixture ' in a German instrument, and it colours the whole organ like a flash of lightning.'' He might have added that when you draw such a stop in an ordinary English organ it generally adds either a screech or " a little mild effervescence on the top," as Casson put it.

The boldest specimen of Schulze's Diapason is the No. 1 Open on the Great at St. Mary's, Tyne Dock, which is metal throughout. More than one English builder has endeavoured to copy it, with varying success, and examples have occasionally been added to existing organs without any regard for proportion or surrounding circumstances. About this period, two well-known English builders attempted to supply bolder Diapason work and chorus. They were J. W. Walker and T. C. Lewis. The latter, an ardent disciple of Schulze, will be referred to shortly. Walker, however, proceeded on somewhat different lines by using larger scales and heavier wind pressures—4 inches or more. His Diapasons were more numerous, weightier, and not nearly so brilliant as Schulze's. They were, however, more in accordance with English tastes and were greatly admired by some. His flue chorus was bold and often well developed, but relatively less powerful than Schulze's, and, like him, he seldom included the tierce. The Walker chorus was most fully exploited in the well-known instrument at Holy Trinity, Sloane Street, London, S.W., built in 1891. Here, the Great and Swell had each two compound stops. The first was of normal type, while the second, called " Clarion Mixture," of considerably greater power, was substituted for the usual 4-ft. reed. As might have been expected, such bold treatment could not be maintained in the treble, and, to make matters worse, the light-pressure chorus reeds were of the old strident type. Nevertheless, with the organ in a somewhat retired position, the full Great fluework without reeds, in that large, resonant building, sounded very imposing. Though quite different in treatment, the effect was somewhat reminiscent of Armley. In the reconstruction of 1935, the old reeds were revoiced on modern lines, and much improvement in their general tone was effected. New 4-ft. reeds were added but, unfortunately, the Clarion Mixtures were done away with; consequently, one of the most characteristic and thrilling effects of the old organ was sacrificed. More unfortunately, the fine church and its organ were much damaged by enemy action. In the later organ at St. Margaret's, Westminster (1897), by the same builders, designed by Lemare, the flue chorus was more normal, but, in that church, Clarion Mixtures would have been out of place. The so-called Double Open Diapason on the Great is really a dull Flute, open to tenor A, the lower part being stopped. Here again, the Great reeds are on light wind. The Swell reeds, however, are on 7 inches, so that better quality is obtained. There is a very large Open Diapason which is a fine stop in itself, but quite out of place in the full Swell. Both manuals include Clarions. If the reeds were modernised, as at Sloane Street, much improvement might be effected, especially on the Great.

Willis's great English contemporary, T. C. Lewis, was the most eminent and consistent of Schulze's disciples in this country, and in much of his best work he followed his methods of voicing. In both cases there was a disproportionate falling-off of power in the trebles ; a fault which Willis always guarded against. As a rule, Lewis also adhered to the older type of chorus reed, and he was at the time its most successful exponent in this country. His finest work was accomplished, almost at the end of his career, in the splendid instrument at Southwark Cathedral, which he built in 1897. The magnificent Great fluework, which culminates in two compound stops, comprising nine ranks, including a complete Cornet, was an emphatic protest against all that Hope Jones stood for. Unfortunately, it fell on deaf ears, as the emasculated flue chorus at Lincoln Cathedral, 1898, Norwich Cathedral, 1899, and York Minster, 1901, proved only too well. It is true that there is a diminutive light-pressure Great Trumpet at Southwark. Fortunately, it cuts no ice, and would have been much more appropriate as a Choir organ chorus reed. This splendid fluework Great would have formed an admirable foil to a set of Willis chorus reeds. Such a possibility did not seem to have occurred to anyone at that time, though something of the kind had been tried by Michell & Thynne in their exhibition organ, built in 1885, which eventually went to Tewkesbury Abbey.

One of the earliest authorities to return to the Great tonal structure was Thomas Casson. He showed that, by making the harmonic series complete, including not only the tierce but the septième (as Cavaillé-Coll had previously done), a satisfactory ensemble for the full Great could be built up without the inclusion of a single chorus reed. Moreover, he demonstrated this practically in one or two medium-sized instruments. Since Casson's day the full harmonic series (including the seventeenth and flat twenty-first) has been one of the most striking features in the tonal design of nearly every important Great Organ built or rebuilt by that great artist, the late Arthur Harrison, from St. Nicholas, Whitehaven, in 1904, onwards. In fact, Harrison's tonal schemes were the exact antithesis of all that Hope Jones advocated. In such cases, chorus reeds are an adjunct ; not a necessity. If moderately smooth, they can combine with the Diapason work. If conservative in power, they are unobtrusive, and so do not upset the Diapason quality. Consequently, the essential flue character is preserved, even in full Great—a matter of vital importance.

Having dealt with the chorus work at some length, a few words must be said about the so-called sub-foundation. So far as doubles are concerned, the continental builders long ago recognised their importance, and also the usefulness of the manual 32-ft. In fact, it has been stated, with some show of reason, that they seemed to build up their Great Organ tonal structure on a 16-ft. rather than on an 8-ft. foundation. Until about 70 years ago, English builders

hardly realised the value of 16-ft. stops on the Great Organ—
even now, it is unusual to find a double in this department
till it reaches nine or ten speaking registers. Excepting
Hereford, not one of Willis's numerous cathedral organs
contained more than a single 16-ft. flue stop on the Great,
but most of them included the not indispensable 16-ft. reed.
The earliest manual 32-ft. stop in England was inserted by
Lincoln at St. Olave's, Southwark, in 1844. An odd specimen
occasionally appeared in instruments by continental makers,
as in Schulze's Doncaster organ. Casson re-introduced the
short compass 32-ft. in one or two instances ; but it is doubtful whether he regarded it as a useful Great Organ register,
or merely inserted it as a means of providing a light double
for the Choir Organ, which he obtained by octave duplication.
In the present century, the inclusion of such a stop on the
Great Organ has been less uncommon, and probably about
a dozen examples exist in more important instruments.
At least half of these occur in organs by Arthur Harrison.
In order to illustrate the points already discussed, the tonal
scheme of the Ely Cathedral Great Organ may be given.
Though by no means the largest, it is the most complete,
for its size, of any Cathedral Great in this country, and set
the standard for Arthur Harrison's designs for many years
to come. To his genius we owe the most important advances
which have been made in tonal structure during the present
century.

ELY CATHEDRAL GREAT ORGAN
(*Harrison and Harrison*, 1908)   19 STOPS

			ft.
Sub-Bordun (throughout) ...	...	... Wood	32
Contra Clarabella ...	... ...	... Wood	16
Gross Geigen	...	... Metal	16
Hohl Flöte (open throughout) ...		... Wood	8

						ft.
Geigen	...	...	...	...	Metal	8
Open Diapason, small	...	...	...	Metal	8
Open Diapason, medium	...	...	...	Metal	8
Open Diapason, large	...	...	...	Metal	8
Quint	...	...	...	...	Wood	5⅓
Wald Flöte (triangular)	...	...	...	Wood	4
Geigen Principal	...	...	...	...	Metal	4
Octave	...	...	...	...	Metal	4
Octave Quint	...	...	...	...	Metal	2⅔
Superoctave ...	...	...	...	...	Metal	2
Harmonics, 10, 17, 19, ♭21, 22		...	Metal	V
Mixture, 15, 19, 22, 26, 29		...	...	Metal	V
Trombone	...	...	...	...	Metal	16
Tromba	...	...	...	...	Metal	8
Octave Tromba	...	...	...	...	Metal	4

Transfer Coupler—Reeds on Orchestral.

Wind Pressures : Flue-work 4½ in.; Reeds 12 in.

NOTE : The three distinct tonal families in the flue-work : Flutes, Geigens, and Diapasons, and the two five-rank compound stops.

It is interesting to compare this with Schulze's Doncaster scheme of 1862. In contrasting the tonal effect, allowance must, of course, be made for the changes which have come about in the style of fluework, and for the revolution which has been achieved in the development of modern reed-voicing methods, which Willis introduced.

Impressive though the general effect of a large, massed Great Organ undoubtedly is, little of it is available for use during the ordinary cathedral daily services. Of recent years, a development in quite another direction has been introduced, and a similar amount of material has been utilised to provide two complete and independent Great Organs, entirely different in tonal structure and character, and available for quite different purposes. One of these is transferable to another manual. There is nothing new in this, for some eighty years ago, two independent Great Organs were provided by Henry Smart and W. T. Best in their designs for the large instruments at Leeds Town Hall and St. Andrew's Hall, Glasgow. In later reconstructions, the advantages these distinguished men foresaw were thrown away, when the independent departments were actually merged into one unwieldy Great Organ! The idea of a divided Great was revived in the reconstruction of the instrument at Norwich Cathedral in 1939. Except for the beautifully conceived Echo Organ, played from a separate manual, the original instrument was a very orthodox four-manual, built in 1899 by Messrs. Norman and Beard, at a time when flue chorus work was under a cloud—nay, had well-nigh reached its nadir. Like Lincoln, the year before, and York a short time after, the flue choruses, as Casson so well put it, were of the " hope I don't intrude " order. The instrument contained many beautifully voiced individual stops, and some fine reed work. It was badly damaged by fire in 1938, which made reconstruction imperative. Fortunately, the opportunity was embraced of making it the most advanced of all our cathedral instruments, so far as the tonal scheme was concerned. The reconstruction was undertaken by Messrs. Hill, Norman & Beard. The Great Organ design is as follows :—

Primary Division 12 Stops	Secondary Division 9 Stops	Wind Pressures
ft.	*ft.*	
Sub-Bordun (ten. C) ... 32	Lieblich Bordun 16	Primary Flue-work : 6 inch
Double Open Diapason ... 16	Contra Dulciana 16	
	Hohl Flöte ... 8	Primary Reeds : 10 inch
Open Diapason, medium ... 8	Geigen ... 8	
	Open Diapason 8	Secondary : 3¼ inch
Open Diapason, large ... 8	Stopped Flute... 4	
Quint ... 5⅓	Geigen Principal 4	
Octave ... 4	Fifteenth ... 2	
Octave Quint... 2⅔	Sesquialtera, 12,	
Superoctave ... 2	15, 17, 19, 22 V	
Mixture, 15, 19, 22, 26 ... IV		
	Transfer Coupler :	
Trombone ... 16	Great Secondary on Choir	
Tromba ... 8		
Clarion ... 4		

Of the two, the secondary division is the more interesting, and in some ways the most important. It is situated in a favourable position on the screen, and consists of light, transparent-toned flue-work of the early Willis type. Unlike the ordinary Cathedral Great, free use can be made of it during the weekday choir services. Moreover, it can be transferred to, and made playable from, the Choir Organ keys. In this way, a large Positive Organ is provided, making an admirable foil to the bolder tone of the Primary Great, a feature most useful in playing Bach and other German composers. The Primary Great is placed in the nave triforium, and is useful for Voluntary playing and recital work. It consists almost entirely of boldly-voiced modern Diapason work, the chorus being surmounted by a family of heavy-pressure reeds. Another admirable example of a divided Great, in a very much smaller three-manual organ, is to be found at Brompton Parish Church, London, S.W. It was built by Messrs. Kingsgate, Davidson & Co. Here, the Primary Great consists of 8, 4, II (12, 15), IV (19, 22, 26, 29), voiced on Schulze lines. It can be transferred to the third manual. The Secondary Great, by contrast, is much milder. It comprises 16, 8, 8, 8, 4, 2⅔, 2, IV (19, 22, 26, 29). There are no reeds in either department. Out of the total of twelve speaking stops, there are no fewer than twelve ranks of chorus work above 4-ft. pitch.

The Swell Organ

Next in importance of the manual departments of the English organ is the Swell. Except Cavaillé-Coll in his latter days, the continental builders did not treat the Swell seriously. The Germans, including Schulze, almost despised it. They considered the Choir, and even the unenclosed Echo, of more importance. This is reflected in their great composers for the organ, such as Rheinberger, Max Reger and even Karg-Elert. Where crescendos are indicated, the " Rollschweller " or " Walze " crescendo is generally pre-supposed, rather than the Swell box. The Swell as we know it is a peculiarly English development, and one of the most important contributions this country has made to organ-building. It was introduced into the organ by Jordan about 1712, and in its original form was an Echo Organ of short compass. Apart from this defect, the early English Swells generally suffered from a muddy 16-ft. register—usually a Stopped Diapason or Bourdon—indifferent flue chorus-work and bad reeds. The combination of the two latter nearly always produced the characteristic " sausage-frying " effect already referred to. One of the earliest Swells with complete compass was made by Willis for his first cathedral organ at Gloucester in 1847, and the tonal development of this department owes more to his genius than that of any other builder. A few of the earlier Swells included the 16-ft. reed as a second double, but it was never inserted without the flue 16-ft. stop to give it body and cover its defects. The first step towards modern design was made in 1861, and a momentous one it was, because it foreshadowed the building up of the Swell tonal structure on a *reed* rather than a *flue* work foundation. In the scheme for a very fine and complete two-manual instrument built by Willis in that year, W. T. Best had the boldness to dispense with the flue double in the Swell altogether, and substitute a Contra Fagotto 16-ft. Though there was no heavy wind, it is worth while to give the design, if only to show how wonderfully modern his conception of the essential features of the Swell really was.

WALLASEY SWELL ORGAN
(Willis, 1861—designed by W. T. Best)

	ft.			ft.
Stopped Diapason ...	8	Contra Fagotto ...	16
Open Diapason ...	8	Oboe	8
Harmonic Flute ...	4	Trumpet	8
Principal	4	Vox Humana ...	8
Mixture	III	Tremulant	
		Octave Coupler	

He clearly saw then how indispensable the 16-ft. reed was to the tonal structure of the Swell, and that no flue stop could act as an effective substitute. Many years were to pass before this was properly understood and recognised; nowadays, it is almost a commonplace. Leaving out of account St. George's Hall, Liverpool, which stood by itself, the next important advance was made at St. Paul's Cathedral in 1872. Here again, the genius of Willis must be given full credit, for he carried out Best's ideas, as exhibited at Wallasey, to their logical conclusion. He entirely reversed the ordinary method of tone-building, and utilised as the foundation a complete family of splendid chorus reeds voiced on heavy wind pressure. The flue-work, though not without its use, was quite subsidiary and, except for the beautifully balanced compound stop, may be omitted from the full Swell without loss—nay, even with positive gain. This Swell, which remains practically as it was in 1872, though not very big, can hold its own with almost any modern example. In most of his larger instruments Willis followed the same general plan, except that the 16-ft. reed was often on the light wind. Sometimes the Mixture was omitted, as at St. Paul's, Knightsbridge; occasionally, for some obscure reason, two Open Diapasons were included (as at Lincoln), but the second 8-ft. chorus reed was very seldom inserted. The tonal scheme of the St. Paul's Swell has nevertheless remained a model on which most of the modern developments have been based. Some builders, it is true, introduced heavy-pressure Diapasons "just to balance the reeds," but such registers are quite foreign to the genius of the true full Swell effect, the chief characteristics of which are reediness and sparkling brilliancy.

In 1885 a very remarkable *multum in parvo* instrument by the short-lived firm of Michell and Thynne appeared at the Inventions Exhibition, and rightly attracted a good deal of attention. It eventually found its way, as a slightly larger four-manual, to Tewkesbury Abbey. Fuller reference will be made to it later, but the Swell must be mentioned here. It is about the same size as Wallasey and, like it, is noteworthy in having for its only double a reed, but this time a Contra Posaune, which, together with the 8-ft. Horn, is on heavy pressure. The Clarion, unfortunately, was only "prepared for." As at St. Paul's, the flue-work, except the Mixture, is quite subsidiary. Shortly after this, Willis built a small four-manual organ with two consoles for St. George's Hall, Windsor Castle. Here again, the only double in the Swell was a reed, a Contra Oboe. Unfortunately, the chorus is almost non-existent, being represented by a solitary 4-ft. Gemshorn. Consequently, with no Mixture or Clarion, the true full Swell effect was not possible. As a contrast the instrument he built for St. Bees Priory Church in 1899, right at the end of his career, may be referred to. Once more, the only double in the Swell is a reed; a most completely satisfying full Swell combination is available, consisting of five stops only : Flageolet 2-ft., Mixture III, Contra Posaune 16-ft., Cornopean 8-ft. and Clarion 4-ft. These three magnificent reeds are on 7-inch wind and very moderate in scale. Like St. Paul's, this full Swell effect is one of thrilling grandeur.

This brings us to the present century. The introduction of the 16-ft. reed as the *first* double in the Swell, and building its tonal structure on a reed foundation was then exploited by Arthur Harrison. Other builders gradually took kindly to it, and at the present time it is quite usual. Another development was the tendency to introduce a chorus of Trumpets of a more fiery quality than the milder Cornopean type which Willis affected, particularly during the latter part of his career. This plan has the advantage, not only of providing an effective contrast with the smoother-toned Great chorus reeds, but, still more important, of securing a wider contrast between the ensembles of the full Swell and full Great which was often lacking in the normal Willis organ, especially when the 16-ft. reed was included in the latter department. Where the Great is reedless, the Willis Cornopean type in the Swell is quite appropriate. A fitting illustration of the points discussed is the magnificent Swell at Ely Cathedral.

ELY CATHEDRAL SWELL ORGAN
(*Harrison and Harrison*, 1908)

		ft.			ft.
Lieblich Bordun...	Wood	16	Oboe	Metal	8
Echo Gamba ...	Metal	8	Vox Humana ...	Metal	8
Voix Céleste			Tremulant		
(Ten. C)	Metal	8	Double Trumpet	Metal	16
Lieblich Gedeckt	Metal	8	Trumpet ...	Metal	8
Open Diapason ...	Metal	8	Horn	Metal	8
Lieblich Flöte ...	Wood	4	Quint Horn ...	Metal	5½
Principal ...	Metal	4	Clarion	Metal	4
Fifteenth... ...	Metal	2	Octave Coupler		
Sesquialtera — 12, 17, 19, 22, 26, 29	Metal	VI			

Wind pressures:
Flue-work and L.P. Reeds, 4½ inch; H.P. Reeds, 10 inch.

Note the well-developed compound stop and the five heavy-pressure chorus reeds, including the Quint Horn—the only example in a British cathedral organ, though it sometimes obtained on the continent. As would be expected, it materially enriches the reed ensemble.

The Choir Organ

The older English builders regarded the Choir Organ (like the continental builders did the Positive) as second only in importance to the Great. For a long period it remained a purely accompanimental, unenclosed division with little colour and, except for improved voicing, no department, for a time, underwent fewer changes. Indeed, some comparatively recent specimens approximate rather closely to the older builders' design. The early English examples were characterised by their bright, sprightly tone, which was largely produced by prominent 4-ft. stops. This doubtless gave colour to the theory, attributed to Hopkins, that the older builders regarded 4 ft. and not 8 ft. as the normal pitch of the Choir. For instance, one found a Principal, 4-ft. Flute and Fifteenth supported only by a Stopped Diapason, sometimes in company with a tenor C Dulciana. The Choir reed was usually a Clarinet—a most unsuitable stop for an unenclosed department. The unenclosed Choir Organ is not the place for essentially solo stops (excepting, perhaps, the Tuba) as it is impossible to endow them with the only imitation of expression which the organ can give.

The early English Choirs, like the Great Organs, contained no doubles, while Mixtures and chorus reeds were very rare. Separate choir Mutations were then unknown in this country. On the continent, as in the case of the Great, there were numerous specimens of fully-developed Positives, complete with doubles, Mixtures and chorus reeds, as well as separate Mutations. Here, however, while 16-ft. flue stops appeared in the Choirs of many cathedral organs, it was in concert instruments that Mixtures and chorus reeds were to be found. Separate Mutations were inserted only in comparatively recent years.

There was a fine example of a complete Choir (unenclosed) in a four-manual organ built by Gray & Davison at Bolton Town Hall in 1874, designed by Best. Its eight speaking registers, including a 16-ft. stop, a beautiful five-rank Dulciana Cornet, and a Trumpet. The last stop, however, was not all that could be desired. A complete Choir Organ, such as has been described, is a desideratum where cathedral music, especially of the older type, is performed. The ringing brilliance of the full Great is sometimes called for without its destructive force, and this can only be supplied by its miniature, the complete designed full Choir, unenclosed. Again, the rendering of Bach's works frequently requires bright episodal passages to be played in contrast with the heavier Great Organ. These can be rendered effectively only on a properly designed, unenclosed Choir.* It is, therefore, not a little remarkable that, until this century, no serious attempt was made to develop the Choir to its logical conclusion, in its natural ecclesiastical home. In most cases, we find it topped by a Piccolo and Clarinet. There was, however, one important exception : the Choir Organ by T. C. Lewis at Southwark, in 1897, which comprised a three-rank Mixture (15, 19, 22). It was the only cathedral organ for many years which contained a compound stop in the Choir. The double was a Lieblich Bordun. Like his magnificent fluework Great Organ, the Lewis Choir fell on deaf ears, and it was not till some ten years later that the real development began.

---

* For the re-introduction of divided Great Organs see *ante* page 86, *et sequa.*

About this time, another change took place. Under the influence of Audsley, the apostle of enclosure, Choirs were placed in swell boxes. Cavaillé-Coll had enclosed a few of his Positifs, and sporadic attempts had been made in this country. The first English Choir, including a double, to be completely enclosed, was that in the well-known organ at St. Margaret's, Westminster, in 1896. The double was a Quintatön and it differed from the ordinary Choir in possessing a certain amount of colour which made it more effective in a box than might have been expected. It was topped by a Piccolo and two orchestral reeds, both 8-ft. The compound stop and chorus reed were absent and the unenclosed Tuba is still prepared for. The next completely enclosed example (with a 16-ft. Salicional) was at St. Bees' Priory (Willis, 1899), similar in size and composition, but here there is, in addition, a fine unenclosed Tuba.

While the enclosure of the Choir Organ may present certain advantages, it undoubtedly reduces its effect to that of a miniature Swell, often merely duplicating its softer effects. It is of little use in Bach playing, as a foil to the Great, since it is too feeble, even with the box wide open.

The real improvements in the tonal structure of the Choir have been effected during the present century and, with one exception, are the results of Arthur Harrison's pioneer work. At Carlisle Cathedral, in 1907, a beautiful little Cornopean was inserted as a Choir chorus reed in place of the Clarinet, which was relegated to the Solo. The double is a Salicional. Unfortunately, room could not be found for a compound stop. At Ely, in 1908, an unenclosed Choir of nine stops, complete from an open 16-ft. Salicional to a three-rank Mixture (12, 19, 22) appeared. It is on only $2\frac{1}{2}$-inch wind, but very boldly voiced. Unfortunately, the

8-ft. and 4-ft. chorus reeds, on 5-inch wind, originally proposed, never materialised. Another fine example of Harrison's work is the enclosed Choir at All Saints', Margaret Street, London, W., which is complete from 16-ft. Contra Dulciana to a five-rank Dulciana Cornet (12, 15, 17, 19, 22) and chorus reed. In a comparatively small church, as All Saints' is, there is some excuse for enclosure. It would make a beautiful Echo Organ in a large building. An interesting design for a nine-stop Choir is that by the late Dr. Alfred Hollins, built in 1916 by Norman and Beard, for Johannesburg Town Hall. It contains an open 16-ft. Salicional and a family of tapered stops, surmounted by a three-rank Cornet (12, 15, 17) and a chorus reed. A very complete scheme is the unenclosed Choir Organ at Brompton Oratory, London ; a composite instrument which contains stops by several builders. The upperwork has recently been added by Messrs. Kingsgate, Davidson & Co., Ltd., to the design of Mr. Ralph Downes, the present organist. The Great Organ is equally rich in flue chorus.

CHOIR ORGAN, BROMPTON ORATORY, LONDON, S.W.
UNENCLOSED.   3¼-INCH WIND.

	ft.
Bourdon	16
Flauto Traverso	8
Stopped Diapason	8
Bell Gamba	8
Principal	4
Flute	4
Quint Flute	2⅔
Octave	2
Tierce	1⅗
Larigot	1⅓
Plein Jeu, 22, 26, 29	III
Zimbel, 33, 36, 40	III

In judging the effect of this particular example, it must be borne in mind that the entire instrument suffers from its confined position. In addition, the Choir Organ has a somewhat unsteady wind supply. These incidental shortcomings, however, do not detract from the remarkable completeness of the tonal design. Indeed, it may be fairly described as a miniature Great Organ. Particular attention is called, not only to the presence of chorus and Diapason Mixtures, but also to the larger-scaled, separate, solo Mutations. These, owing to their relatively prominent foundation tone, are particularly useful as they produce *quasi*-synthetic effects for melodic purposes. On the other hand, they are not so satisfactory as part of the chorus, for which breaking compound stops composed of smaller-scaled pipes are necessary.

Credit for the re-introduction into this country of separate solo Mutations must be given to Messrs. Willis & Sons Ltd. This firm has brought them into use since about 1925. They are made of stopped, large Gemshorn, and normal Flute pipes. In addition to the pitches already given, the septième, or flat twenty-first, and the twenty-second may also be included. The question of whether to enclose the Choir Organ is somewhat difficult. If it is designed as a Secondary Great it should certainly not be enclosed ; otherwise, its special character vanishes. Many Choir Organs, originally voiced for the open, have been ruined by enclosure, especially in large buildings, where they have often been reduced to mere Echo Organs. On the other hand, if a highly-coloured orchestral department, containing solo registers, is desired, it must be voiced on heavier wind and be much more positive in tone ; but this will be dealt with later. In large instruments it is sometimes possible to have two independent departments, played from one manual. Probably the most advanced design of this kind is at Norwich Cathedral, where the lowest manual has two separate departments.

NORWICH CATHEDRAL CHOIR ORGAN
(*Hill, Norman and Beard,* 1940)
POSITIVE ORGAN (unenclosed, 2½-inch wind)
CHOIR ORGAN (enclosed, 4-inch wind)

	ft.		ft.
Quintatön	16	Violoncello	8
Contra Dulciana ...	16	Dolce	8
Chimney Flute ...	8	Cor de Nuit... ...	8
Bell Gamba	8	Unda Maris (Ten. C)	
Dulciana	8	(Flute Céleste) ...	8
Nason Flute ...	4	Gemshorn	4
Principal	4	Nazard	2⅔
Twelfth	2⅔	Flageolet	2
Fifteenth	2	Schalmei	16
Tierce	1⅗	Trumpet	8
Harmonics	III		

19, ♮21, 22

The Echo Organ

Of this department little need be said. In England, it was originally the precursor of the Swell, by which it was gradually replaced. In more recent times, it has re-appeared, sometimes under fancy names, producing, for the most part, purely fancy effects. Until recently, the Echo Organ in America was almost a *sine qua non.* Lately it has become less common, though it sometimes appears in larger instruments. The mystery with which it is commonly associated is much enhanced by the retired position it normally occupies, often at some distance from the main organ. In German instruments it was looked upon more seriously. It was generally designed as a smaller and softer edition of the

Positive department, on lighter wind, and on an open sound-board. It formed the third manual. Schulze left some fine specimens in this country, of which the beautiful example at Armley is typical. The scheme is complete from a light double to a subdued Twelfth and Fifteenth. The wind pressure is but 1½ inches. Some of the stops are mere whispers, and their delicate voicing is easily disturbed by dust. An Echo Organ, to be really effective, requires much bolder treatment, a moderate wind pressure, and enclosure in a box. There is a large one, divided into two sections, by Messrs. Hill (1895) at Westminster Abbey. There is also a smaller, but excellent specimen at the extreme east end of Norwich Cathedral.

NORWICH CATHEDRAL ECHO ORGAN
(*Norman, Beard*, 1899)

	ft.		ft.
Sub-Bass (12 pipes only for pedal effects)	16	Viola	4
Contra Viola	16	Harmonic Piccolo ...	2
Gamba	8	Cornet	VI
Zauberflöte	8	Harmonic Trumpet...	8
Unda Maris (Flute Céleste, Ten. C)	8	Vox Humana ...	8
Vox Angelica (two ranks) ...	8	Tremulant	
		Octave Coupler	

ENCLOSED, 6-inch wind.

Perhaps its most noteworthy features are a beautiful six-rank Cornet and Harmonic Trumpet. Neither of these Echo Organs has been connected up since the latest rebuilds. Such departments are pure luxuries, as all desirable Echo effects can easily be produced from the ordinary Swell or enclosed Choir. Indeed, many of the latter departments would make excellent Echo organs.

The Solo and Orchestral Organ

Like the Swell, the Solo Organ is a purely English department, and, as its name implies, it was originally a division confined to registers of a pronounced solo character, thrown together haphazard, without any idea of ensemble effects ; still less of building up a tonal structure. It was, indeed, a fortuitous concourse of atoms, and in one or two instances the fourth manual had but two stops, an Harmonic Flute and a Tromba ! Now, the brothers Willis were again pioneers. In 1855 a Solo Organ of 15 stops was actually constructed by them at St. George's Hall, Liverpool, comprising ten splendid reeds. Some time later, Henry's gifted son Vincent began the development of loaded reed work on heavier wind pressure, thus laying the foundation of modern reed voicing with which the name and fame of Willis will be associated for ever. In 1867, at Best's instigation, he raised the pressure of the four heavy reeds from $9\frac{1}{2}$ to 22 inches, thereby producing Tuba effects of a thrilling grandeur never before conceived. In 1899 the flue-work and orchestral reeds were enclosed in a Swell box, but the four Tubas were left outside. But we are anticipating. In 1872 a six-stop Solo was inserted in St. Paul's Cathedral, and as this was to be the standard type for his many cathedral instruments for some time to come, it is worth while to give the Scheme as it then stood.

	ft.			ft.
Flûte Harmonique ...	8	Tuba Magna	...	8
Concert Flute ...	4	Tuba Clarion	...	4
Corno di Bassetto ...	8			
Orchestral Oboe ...	8			

Wind Pressures :

Flue-work ...	...	...	4-inch
Orchestral reeds	...	...	3½-inch
Tubas :			
Bass	...	...	14-inch
Treble ...	...	...	17½-inch

It was, of course, entirely unenclosed. There were two additional orchestral reeds of 8-ft. pitch on the open sound-board of the Choir, a Cor Anglais and another Corno di Bassetto. Two points are worthy of note : no attempt was made to impart gradation of tone to any of the orchestral stops—a feature now almost universally insisted upon—and not one of the four orchestral reeds was of 16-ft. pitch, in spite of the fact that the Corno di Bassetto was duplicated. As a consequence, such delightful combinations as Bassoon 16-ft., Clarinet 8-ft. and Flute 4-ft. were impossible. Gamba tone, too, was absent, and the modern Viol was yet undreamt of, though it was more than foreshadowed by the vivid colouring of the Willis Orchestral Oboe.

About 1898, towards the end of his wonderful career, a great advance was made, both at St. Paul's, and at Lincoln Cathedral, by the enclosure of most of the Solo department except the Tubas. A 16-ft. orchestral reed appeared at Lincoln, but on the unenclosed Choir ; and another was inserted in the new Solo at St. Paul's. Incidentally, the feature of the enclosed Solo, or perhaps of the whole organ, not excepting the 25-inch pressure Dome Tubas, was the wonderful pair of small-scaled Trumpets, 16-ft. and 8-ft. pitch, on 17½-inch wind, which were voiced by Vincent Willis. These were, alas, almost destroyed by enemy action, but have now been reconstructed. Though no attempt was made, in either case, to build up a definite ensemble or tonal structure, it is interesting to note the germ of the modern String tone family which was in the enclosed Altar Organ at that time.

Soon after the beginning of the present century, Arthur Harrison once more proved himself to be the pioneer. He boldly replaced the purely solo organ by an enclosed department, where ensemble effects of a definite character were paramount. At the same time, the ordinary orchestral solo registers were not only present, but were even built up into the tonal structure. The latter were, however, a secondary consideration. The ensemble was based upon a foundation of Flutes and Strings—a development of Cavaillé-Coll's Flûte Harmonique and Gambe combination. A 16-ft. stop was invariably included, and an entire harmonic structure, in complete contrast with any other department of the organ. It gave an endless variety of charming ensemble effects of which the ordinary Solo Organ was absolutely incapable. A department possessing such rich colouring and varied functions is appropriately termed "Orchestral" rather than "Solo." These ideas were put into practice on a considerable scale in Harrison's first complete cathedral organ at Carlisle, in 1907. Here, they are exemplified by the beautiful fourth manual department, which is replete with colour. Not long after this, in his next cathedral instrument, at Ely, they were revealed to the world fully developed.

Ely Cathedral Orchestral Organ
(*Harrison and Harrison*, 1908)

ENCLOSED SECTION—				ft.
6-inch wind :	ft.	*Clarinet		16
Contra Viola	... 16	Orchestral Oboe	...	8
Viole d'Orchestre	... 8	Tremulant		
Viole Céleste ...	... 8			
Viole Octaviante	... 4			
Cornet de Violes (10,		UNENCLOSED, 20-inch wind :		
12, 15) ...	... III	Tuba	...	8
Harmonic Flute	... 8	Octave		
Harmonic Flute	... 4	Sub-octave		
Harmonic Piccolo	... 2	Unison off		

It is, of course, well known that the complete family of strings was strongly advocated by Audsley. Although this design was conceived forty years ago, it embodies most of the important features which have been included since. In more recent times, separate Mutation ranks (mentioned above) have come into use. Attempts have also been made to imitate the elusive tone of the French Horn.† The difficulty lies in the very extensive difference of timbre exhibited by the instrument between piano and forte playing. More or less successful imitations have been produced by Messrs. Willis, Rushworth and Dreaper, Compton, and by Harrison, in 16 and 8-ft. pitch. These exhibit the modern technique of reed voicing, and give a fair imitation of the Horn in its *mezzo* register. They are, however, so smooth in tone that in a spacious building they are almost indistinguishable from flue stops. As they are very expensive to produce it is, therefore open to question whether the game is worth the candle. At the other end of the scale is the "Trompette

---

* A piston labelled " Clarinet 8-ft. " draws Clarinet 16-ft., Octave Coupler and Unison off.

† Even this was tried by Willis at the Albert Hall as long ago as 1872 !

Militaire," with tubes of spun brass, inserted by Messrs. Willis in the St. Paul's Cathedral organ during the reconstruction about 1933.

With suitable modifications, an orchestral department is sometimes preferred to the unenclosed, or purely accompanimental Choir Organ in a three-manual instrument. In this connection, it is interesting to note that as far back as 1877 in Ouseley's design for the three-manual Willis at the Sheldonian Theatre, Oxford, the Choir was omitted. The third manual was an unenclosed Solo Organ, and, for the first time, included a Tuba. The importance of this has been fully recognised in recent years. The same arrangement was followed by Willis in his 1885 Exhibition organ. This was re-erected as a four-manual in Canterbury Cathedral, with electro-pneumatic action throughout, and was reconstructed and enlarged by Messrs. Willis in 1948.

The Tuba and Bombard Organ

This subsidiary department takes its first name from that commanding register, the true development of which will be for ever associated with the name of Willis, though it was originally introduced by another. We have already seen how his son Vincent was associated with Best in the great advance which was made at St. George's Hall, Liverpool, in 1867. It was the latter who, in his compositions, his arrangements, and most of all in his playing, first proved conclusively the predominant value of reed tone of pure, even quality which could be used *alone*, in contrast with, and apart from, rather than in conjunction with, the Great organ flue-work. In fact, his use of the Tuba and other heavy reeds in that manner was nothing short of masterly, and in this respect he has never been approached by any composer or organ player. But if Willis's superb specimens of reed voicing had not been available Best's conceptions of registration would have been impossible of realisation ; to attempt them would have been to court disaster. It may be said without exaggeration that in voicing heavy-pressure reeds in general, and Tubas in particular, Willis and his son outdistanced all their rivals and made one of England's greatest contributions to the organ-building world.

If such powerful reeds are not available on another manual apart from the Great Organ, they lose most of their value. They form no part of the tonal structure of any department, except in the rare instances when they can make up one of their own. A Tuba Organ of five stops—16-ft., 8-ft., 8-ft., 4-ft., 4-ft., on pressures varying from $14\frac{1}{2}$ to 25 inches—appeared as a fifth manual in the 1898 reconstruction at St. Paul's Cathedral. There is a similar department, with higher pressures (also on the fifth manual) at Liverpool Cathedral (Willis, 1924). Both are entirely unenclosed and the latter includes a Grand (flue) Chorus of 10 ranks, on 10-inch wind.

It is doubtful whether, for concentrating the brass into one group, the awkwardly placed fifth manual is necessary or desirable.

In the ordinary three-manual organ it has been customary for a long time to voice the Great chorus reeds as semi-Tubas, and make them transferable to another manual for quasi-Tuba effects. This was done by Norman & Beard, at the late Dr. Rootham's instigation, at St. John's College, Cambridge, in 1902, and was a feature in all Harrison's instruments of importance. It has since become almost a commonplace.

So far, only unenclosed Tubas have been dealt with. Many authorities, however, have held, with some show of reason, that an enclosed Tuba should be the primary consideration, on the grounds that it can be used more freely. On the other hand, there can be no doubt that the normal stop loses much of its characteristic tone quality and brilliant splendour by enclosure. Even under the most favourable circumstances its essential feature—the commanding effect against the bigger combinations of the Great Organ—is generally destroyed. As many modern examples are smoother than the Willis type, this argument applies *a fortiori*. Conversely, the more blatant kind, with open reeds, are vastly improved by enclosure ; indeed, in most cases it is only under such circumstances that their effect is tolerable, unless the building be very resonant. This leads us to a consideration of a further development in modern times called the Bombard department, from the French "*Clavier des Bombardes.*" It has a tonal structure consisting of a complete family of heavily-winded reeds and a very powerful compound stop—enclosed, of course, in a Swell box. The germ of the idea was contained in the St. Paul's Cathedral Swell of 1872, but it is doubtful if Willis ever appreciated its significance. To T. C. Lewis must be given the credit for first clearly recognising the potentiality of such a department—really a super full Swell. In his *multum in parvo* design for the organ at the People's Palace, Mile End Road, London, E., such a division, playable separately from the Swell and Great keys, was inserted about 1886. It consisted of a family of 16-ft., 8-ft. and 4-ft. chorus reeds and two Mixtures, all on 12-inch wind. It was perhaps the first instance of a set of heavy-pressure reeds being made available independently on two different manuals—a valuable device of which the modern builder has taken full advantage.

Incidentally, it is worthy of note that Lewis usually enclosed his heavy reeds.

The Bombard division was strongly advocated by the late Carlton C. Michell (of Michell & Thynne) and was inserted by him in two or three organs in America. With one exception, it hardly exists in complete form in this country. The late Dr. Alfred Hollins included it in his fine design for Johannesburg Town Hall.

JOHANNESBURG TOWN HALL BOMBARD ORGAN
(*Norman and Beard*, 1916)
ALL ENCLOSED ON 12-INCH WIND

		ft.
Contra Trombone	32
Trombone	16
Harmonic Horn ... ..., ...	8
Trompette Harmonique...	8
Quint Horn	5⅓
Clairon Harmonique	4
Grand Fourniture (12, 15, 19, 22, 26, 29) ...	VI

The department is playable from any or all four manuals. There is, in addition, an unenclosed Tuba (16-inch wind) on the Solo Organ. Note the 32-ft. reed and the Quint Horn. The former was then the only manual example in the world. Of the latter, there were but one or two specimens in this country, though they obtained on the continent. There is a large edition of the Bombard Organ in the Royal Albert Hall, London (1934), by Harrison, but it has no manual 32-ft. reed.

The Pedal Organ

Though this department is treated last, it is second only in importance to the Great Organ itself. For the earliest examples, we must look to the continent, especially to

Germany, where well-developed Pedal Organs have existed for 400 years or more. In England, we had no pedals for centuries after the Germans had developed it so fully, but we eventually had something which they had not, which gave to our bass, clumsy though it was, a dignity and grandeur which no German Pedal ever had, in spite of its brave show on paper. That was our large-scaled, open wood pedal pipes—miscalled Diapason. This stop has been decried by nearly all writers from Hopkins to the present day. Nevertheless, its influence has generally pervaded our pedal designs, and as our Diapason work has always been a feature in our Great Organs, no one would seriously propose to dispense with it. Another almost equally important stop which, later on, greatly enhanced the grandeur of our English Pedal organ, was the full-toned, heavy-pressure 16-ft. reed introduced by Willis. Both these registers contribute to the most impressive features of our modern instruments, but they cannot be found in continental organs.

Of recent years, another prominent pedal stop has been developed, the heavy-pressure Contra Bass, which is a passable imitation of its orchestral namesake. It was foreshadowed by Schulze in the Violone at Hindley. Early specimens were made by Pendlebury (who was in charge of the Hindley organ) and by Whiteley. A somewhat similar stop with a diaphonic bass has been used by Compton. It has, however, been chiefly exploited by Messrs. Willis, both in wood and metal. An excellent specimen of the former was added to the organ at St. George's Hall, Liverpool, in their reconstruction of 1931. A fine example of the latter was inserted by them in the instrument at St. Giles' Cathedral, Edinburgh, which they rebuilt and enlarged in 1940. The large pipes stand in the front and this stop dominates the whole of the Pedal flue-work. It has an 8 and 4-ft. extension. In addition to its use in pedal solos, it acts as a foil to the Open Wood, and gives definition and point to the Pedal organ. A milder type might be useful in smaller instruments where there is not room for the Open Wood. The want of the Pedal in the earlier English organs led to their manual compass being extended down to $10\frac{2}{3}$ ft. G, and even to 16 ft. C. This method, clumsy and expensive though it was, did provide a varied and appropriate bass to the more important manual stops. On the other hand, you may search the pages of Hopkins and Rimbault in vain to find the slightest indication that there was anything at all to be said in favour of long manuals. As a matter of fact, they were ruthlessly swept away, and we adopted independent, and generally miserably inadequate, Pedals. A few of our largest organs were, however, well supplied, such as St. George's Hall, Liverpool (1855), 17 stops; York Minster (1859), 19 stops; and the Albert Hall, London (1871), 21 stops. But during the latter part of the last century a Pedal of four to six stops was, in this country, considered adequate for quite a large instrument. An ordinary three-manual (and sometimes a four-manual) Willis usually contained: Open Wood 16-ft., Bourdon 16-ft. an 8-ft. flue stop and a 16-ft. reed. The Violone (really a 16-ft. Salicional) occasionally appeared as a substitute for, or as an addition to, the Bourdon. In larger instruments, the open 32-ft. and an 8-ft. reed, and sometimes a Mixture were added. Fine as this foundation was, it is obvious that it was conceived in terms of the Great Organ only. There was a want of variety among the softer basses for the other departments, which are more frequently required.

About 1885 a great reformer appeared in Thomas Casson, and to his teaching, more than to anyone else, we owe the fine English Pedal Organs of today. In the first place, he laid down that the function of the Pedal is threefold :-

(1) Primarily, to provide instantaneously an appropriate bass for any combination of manual stops and couplers.

(2) To provide, when required, an obligato bass differing in power and tone from that of the manuals.

(3) An extension of (2), to provide absolute pedal solo effects for the assertion of a melody or subject.

Though the standard Willis Pedal might be able to supply (3) or even (2) to a limited extent, it failed in (1) altogether. At first sight, the provision of a Pedal Organ complete enough to satisfy all these ideals (and who can gainsay them) would be prohibitive in cost and the amount of space required. If it were really necessary to have every stop independent this would undoubtedly be the case. This brings us to the point as to how Casson's ideals can be realised. He himself demonstrated how a Pedal Organ, adequate for the purpose, can be provided economically by means of legitimate and judicious borrowing, though he pointed out that this was no essential part of his theory. Such borrowing used to be regarded with suspicion, but Casson's methods were freely exploited, first by no less a person than Arthur Harrison, and at the present times they are employed by practically all builders, good, bad, and indifferent. In actual practice, the Pedal organ is now made up as follows :—

(1) The most important stops must be independent.

(2) Pedal stops of which the upper and lower ranges, or both, may be borrowed from such independent stops. Nowadays, this is known as " extension."

(3) The upper range of pedal stops may be borrowed from the co-relative manual stops.

   (4) Manual doubles may be borrowed on the Pedal in
       identical pitch. By this means a variety of softer 16-ft.
       basses can be economically obtained.

It should be mentioned that, in recent times, these methods
have been greatly facilitated by the employment of electric
action. Nowadays, when economy is so stringent, the
provision of an entirely independent Pedal Organ can be
regarded only as a counsel of perfection. On the other hand,
the practical advantages of extension and borrowing in this
department are so great, and the artistic losses so slight,
that the very few dissentient voices now raised are hardly
worth serious attention.

One point which Casson considered of great importance
was the provision of enclosed Pedal stops to form the bass
of the Swell or other enclosed departments. This was first
carried out by Harrison in the small three-manual organ
at Clare College, Cambridge, in 1911, where the Pedal reed,
on 7-inch wind, was enclosed in the Swell box, thereby greatly
increasing its usefulness in so small a building. In his
splendid instrument at St. Mary Redcliffe, Bristol, the 32-ft.
and 16-ft. pedal reeds, on 15-inch wind, borrowed from each
other, were enclosed in the Swell chamber. The latter was
destroyed, not by enemy action, but by a madman's arson.*
Harrison adopted the same plan in his reconstruction of the
Royal Albert Hall organ in 1935. A similar arrangement was
carried out by Messrs. Willis at Liverpool Cathedral in 1924.
Opportunities for doing such things are naturally rare, but
quasi-expressive Pedal basses on a small scale can easily
be provided by borrowing enclosed manual doubles on to the
Pedal.

---

* It has now been reconstructed.

A Pedal Organ which aims at completeness must contain the harmonic structure. During the decline of Mixtures such stops, the effect of which was often as coarse and unpleasing as their manual counterparts, naturally also disappeared. Now that increasing attention is being paid to a scientifically built-up and complete tonal structure on the manuals, and less reliance is, rightly, being placed on Pedal couplers, this department cannot logically be left *without*. Much improvement in this respect has taken place in the present century and a fine example is the five-rank Harmonics 12, 17, 19, b21, 22, (the 15th is separate) at Johannesburg Town Hall, 1916. Though it is very boldly voiced its enclosure in one of the Swell boxes renders it most useful in light solo combinations of a special character and in no way detracts from its telling effect in the full. Pedal compound stops will be further considered when we come to deal with the extension organ. Reference has already been made to the Pedal Cornet in Chapter 1. Perhaps the best illustration of the points which have been discussed will be seen in the Pedal Organ at Westminster Abbey, designed by Arthur Harrison in 1937. Unfortunately, he did not live to complete it. In order to show the progress that has been made the old Pedal specification (Hill 1895) will first be given.

	ft.		ft.
Double Open Wood ...	32	Contra Posaune ...	32
Open Wood No. 1 ...	16	Posaune	16
Open Wood No. 2 ...	16	Trumpet	8
Open Diapason ...	16		
Bourdon	16		
Principal	8	Except Open Wood No. 1,	
Bass Flute	8	all Pedal stops were on	
'Cello	8	light wind.	

WESTMINSTER ABBEY PEDAL ORGAN
(*Harrison and Harrison*, 1937)

	ft.		ft.
Double Open Wood ...	32	Fifteenth (20 from Principal)	4
Open Wood No. 1 ...	16	Mixture (12, 17, 19, 22) ...	IV
Open Wood No. 2 (20 from 32-ft.)	16	Clarinet (from solo) ...	16
Open Diapason (Metal)	16	Tuba (from solo) ...	16
Geigen (from Great) ...	16	Double Ophicleide (20 from Ophicleide) ...	32
Viole (from solo) ...	16	Ophicleide	16
Sub-Bass (from Great) ...	16	Posaune (20 from Ophicleide)	8
Dulciana (from Choir) ...	16		
Octave (20 from O.W.1)	8		
Principal (20 from Open Diapason)	8	*Wind pressures :*	
Flute (from Great) ...	8	Flue-work : 3½ to 6 inches.	
		Reeds : 6 to 20 inches.	

Borrowing and extension have been freely resorted to. There are no independent enclosed basses for the Swell but these have been partly provided for by borrowing the enclosed Solo Contra Tuba on to the Pedal. 'Manual doubles have been freely borrowed to provide a variety of softer basses.

The provision of Pedal obligatos and solo effects, already alluded to, must also be considered. Charming obligatos of a light orchestral nature have, in recent times, been rendered possible by borrowing the manual 16-ft. Clarinet, Bassoon, or Cor Anglais where these obtain. While they are effective enough at close quarters, their tone is lost in large buildings, and it is doubtful whether the game is worth the candle. For bolder solo passages, the Swell double reed, or even the heavy-pressure 16-ft. Solo reed, where one exists, may be similarly treated. Where the Great reeds include one of 16-ft. pitch, and they are transferable to another manual, it may also be used as a Pedal solo through the appropriate coupler.

In well-equipped modern instruments, a pronounced solo effect is instantly available by means of a reversible piston acting on the drawstop of the heavy 16-ft. Pedal reed itself. Such a simple device is useful as far as it goes, since it enables a Pedal subject to be brought out when required, and the bass resumed at will.

With the provision of an adequate Pedal tonal scheme such as has been described, the question of efficient control becomes a matter of great importance. It seems somewhat strange that, while Casson's ideas on the function and design of this department have been largely acted upon, his control system has been practically ignored. Yet it undoubtedly saved the player a great deal of purely routine manipulation of Pedal stops and couplers. In fact, he need never have thought about them unless he required some special effect, as proper basses were automatically furnished. If, however, he preferred hand registration, the control could be switched off at any time. In addition, a variety of Pedal solo effects could be prepared, not only in advance, but also introduced and discontinued as required, with the minimum amount of stop manipulation. Nevertheless, players seem to have been content with a device which enables the combination pistons of the various manual departments to provide a suitable Pedal bass when required. This can be extended to the couplers when they are (as Casson insisted they should be) grouped with the drawstops of the departments they augment. These features were fully exploited by Willis at Lincoln in 1898 and St. Bees in 1899. In addition to giving the proper Pedal and Coupler, pistons controlling solo stops gave a suitable accompaniment on another manual. Combination couplers of this kind were extensively used by Harrison and one or two other builders. These have been largely superseded by the second-touch pistons introduced by Messrs. Walker and Messrs. Compton. General pistons controlling the whole organ have also been re-introduced— they were first introduced by Willis at St. George's Hall, Liverpool, as long ago as 1855 !

The further discussion of the question of control is outside the subject of tonal structure, but something more will be said about it in the next chapter.

General

We have now studied each department of the organ separately and shown how it has developed in this country into the most complete form known to us up to the present time. Examples (by no means the largest) have been given by way of illustration. We will now turn our attention to the instrument as a whole, and give some specimens of complete schemes to illustrate particular points to which attention has already been drawn. It is possible that these may be of assistance to those who may be called upon to draw up specifications of instruments of various sizes, about which something more will be said later. So far, the departments of larger organs have been chiefly considered, but it may be useful to start at the other end of the scale. Perhaps the most effective two-manual organ, for its size, ever constructed was the diminutive " Willis on Wheels " (so named because the whole instrument is on a movable platform), built by the master for St. Paul's Cathedral in 1881.

"WILLIS ON WHEELS"—ST. PAUL'S CATHEDRAL
(*Willis*, 1881)

GREAT ORGAN		SWELL ORGAN		PEDAL ORGAN	
ft.			*ft.*		*ft.*
Lieblichgedeckt	8	Open Diapason	8	Bourdon ...	16
Open Diapason	8	Gemshorn ...	4	COUPLERS :	
Principal ...	4	Cornopean ...	8	Swell to Great	
Fifteenth ...	2			Great to Pedals	
				Swell to Pedals	

Tracker action to manuals. Tubular action to pedals.

Tubular action, to the manuals also, was substituted for tracker in 1925.

WIND PRESSURE : $3\frac{1}{2}$ inches.

Note the Great of only four stops to Fifteenth, and the Swell of three stops, including a chorus reed. Each is complete and independent of the Swell to Great coupler. This scheme was the foundation used by the late Mr. F. J. Livesey (for 47 years the accomplished organist of St. Bees Priory Church) in his design for Cleator Parish Church, Cumberland, built by Harrison & Harrison in 1902.

CLEATOR PARISH CHURCH, CUMBERLAND
(*Harrison and Harrison*, 1902)

GREAT ORGAN		SWELL ORGAN		PEDAL ORGAN	
ft.			*ft.*		*ft.*
Double Salicional		Geigen... ...	8	Sub-Bass ...	16
(FFF, 7 stopped)	16	Lieblichflöte ...	4		
Claribel Flute...	8	Cornopean ...	8	COUPLERS :	
Open Diapason	8	Octave Coupler		Great to Pedals	
Principal ...	4			Swell to Pedals	
Fifteenth ...	2				
Swell to Great					

Tracker action to manuals. Tubular action to pedals.

WIND PRESSURE : $3\frac{1}{2}$ inches.

Note the important addition of the Great double and
the Swell octave coupler. The former imparts the dignity
and impressive effect of a much bigger organ, and when
played with the Flute an octave higher, it gives a Choir
Organ effect. This design was much used by Messrs. Harrison
& Harrison in their small church organs which, so far as they
go, are admirable for the accompaniment of congregational
singing.

The counterpart of Cleator is another little instrument
built nearly fifty years later by Messrs. Harrison for the
parish church at Stornoway in the Isle of Lewis.

STORNOWAY CHURCH
(Harrison and Harrison, 1949)

PEDAL ORGAN
(Enclosed in a Swell box)

Sub-Bass	... ...	16
Flute (18 from Sub-Bass)		8
Great to Pedal		
Swell to Pedal		

GREAT ORGAN

Double Salicional (T. C)		16
Rohr Gedeckt	...	8
Open Diapason	...	8
Principal	... ...	8
Swell to Great		

SWELL ORGAN

Hohlflöte	... ...	8
Gamba	... ...	8
Geigen Principal	...	4
Cornet (12, 15, 17)	...	III

3-inch wind pressure.
Tracker action to Great
  and Swell.
Pneumatic action to Pedal.

The inclusion of a Fifteenth on the Great was originally
contemplated but had to be abandoned for lack of funds.
This was unfortunate as the Great ensemble would then have
been complete. The Swell has no reed stop, its place being
taken by a small compound stop, which not only completes
the tonal structure, but gives greater possibilities in combination and even for solo use. It is also more stable in such an
uncertain climate, where tuning facilities are seldom available.

Note the Flute and Gamba in the Swell, which are reminiscent of Cavaillé-Coll.

Another remarkable design by F. J. Livesey, for a church in Wellington, New Zealand, is here given.

WELLINGTON CHURCH, NEW ZEALAND
(*Jardine*, 1912)

PEDAL ORGAN		GREAT ORGAN		SWELL ORGAN	
	ft.		*ft.*		*ft.*
Sub-Bass ...	16	Double Sali-		Viol	8
Flute (18 from		cional ...	16	Stopped Flute	8
Sub-Bass) ...	8	(Ten. C bass		Geigen Principal	4
Open Wood ...	16	from Pedal		Mixture (12, 15,	
Great to Pedal		Sub-Bass)		19, 22) ...	IV
Swell to Pedal		Claribel Flute...	8	Contra Fagotto	16
		Open Diapason	8	Octave Coupler	
		Principal ...	4		
		Twelfth ...	2⅔		
		Fifteenth ...	2	*Wind pressure :*	
		Swell to Great		3¼-inch.	

Tracker action to Great and Swell. Pneumatic action to Pedal.

Note the Great to Fifteenth, the fine Swell with a complete four-rank Mixture, and the 16-ft. Contra Fagotto—the only reed in the organ—and all within a total of only fourteen speaking stops. When Harrison's little instrument for St. Nicholas College, Chislehurst (now in the crypt of Canterbury Cathedral) was built in 1931, it was thought to be most revolutionary as the only double in the organ, and the only reed, was the Swell 16-ft. Contra Oboe. The fact that this had been anticipated by nearly twenty years was overlooked. This instrument has pneumatic action but the other four organs so far described have tracker. This is all that is necessary or desirable for such small instruments, especially in country places where periodical attention is difficult or impossible to obtain. It is extremely durable, and responsive, and the touch need not be objectionably heavy. In certain circumstances, it can be used even for a three-manual where light wind is employed, as at All Hallow's, Twickenham. Here, the tracker action, though seventy years old, was still serviceable, and was retained in the reconstruction for reasons of economy. The original specification was faulty and incomplete, but the pipe-work included five seventeenth-century stops by Renatus Harris, which were, of course, retained. As the old action and sound boards had to be used again, the only feasible changes were accomplished by transposing and altering the pitch of some existing stops. Nevertheless, a sound, if somewhat unconventional, tonal scheme was obtained in a most economical manner. In the Swell, the new Sesquialtera, which replaced a useless tenor C Oboe, is useful in solo combinations, while the Mixture is a chorus stop.

ALL HALLOWS CHURCH, TWICKENHAM
(Rebuilt, Kingsgate, Davidson and Co., 1941)

GREAT ORGAN	ft.	SWELL ORGAN	ft.	CHOIR ORGAN (Enclosed)	ft.
Bordun	16	Stopped Dia-		Viola	8
Claribel Flute	8	pason	8	Stopped Flute	8
Open Diapason	8	Open Diapason	8	Dulciana	8
Nason Flute	4	Principal	4	Dulciana Céleste	
Principal	4	Fifteenth	2	(Ten. C)	8
Twelfth	2⅔	Sesqualtera		Wood Flute	4
Fifteenth	2	(Ten. C), 12, 17	II	Tremulant	
Fourniture —		Mixture 19, 22	II	Swell to Choir	
19, 22, 26	III	Krummhorn	16		
Trumpet	8	Cornopean	8		
Swell to Great					

PEDAL ORGAN

Bordun (from Great)	16
Bordun (from Great)	8
Bordun (from Great)	4
Open Bass (Wood)	16
Octave (18 from Open Bass)	8
Krummhorn (from Swell)	16
Trombone (18 from Great Trumpet)	16
Great to Pedals	
Swell to Pedals	
Choir to Pedals	

Tracker action except for Great Bordun and Trumpet, and Pedal Organ, which have tubular action.

WIND PRESSURE: 3¼ inch.

Note the Swell double reed of Clarinet type, economical alike of space and material. This was used by Harrison in the Swell at Clare College, Cambridge, in 1911, and many other fine examples were subsequently made by him. Before we proceed to larger designs, something must be said about the remarkable *multum in parvo* organ built by Michell & Thynne for the Inventions Exhibition in 1885, the Swell of which has already been alluded to. The tonal scheme, as later re-erected in Tewkesbury Abbey, is as follows:—

TEWKESBURY ABBEY
(*Michell and Thynne*, 1885-7)

PEDAL ORGAN		GREAT ORGAN		SWELL ORGAN	
	ft.		*ft.*		*ft.*
Harmonic Bass	32	Violone ...	16	Open Diapason	8
Great Bass		Open Diapason I	8	Flauto Traverso	8
(Wood) ...	16	Open Diapason II	8	Viole de Gambe	8
Dolce (Open) ...	16	Claribel ...	8	Voix Céleste	
Great Flute		Octave ...	4	(to GG) ...	8
(Open) ...	8	Flûte Octaviante	4	Geigen ...	4
Bombarde ...	16	Rauschquint 12,		Mixture 15, 19,	
Choir to Pedals		15	II	22	III
Great to Pedals		Great Mixture,		Contra Posaune	16
Swell to Pedals		19, 22, 26, 29...	IV	Horn	8
Flue-work :		Trombone ...	16	Oboe	8
3½-inch wind.		Trumpet ...	8	OCTAVE COUPLER	
Reed :		Choir Sub to Great		*Flue-work* :	
10-inch wind.		Swell to Great		3½-inch wind.	
		Solo to Great		*Reeds* :	
SOLO ORGAN		*Flue-work* :		7-inch wind.	
Harmonic Flute	8	3½-inch wind.		CHOIR ORGAN	
Violoncello ...	8	*Reeds and Mixture* :		Spitzflöte ...	8
Voix Humaine		6-inch wind.		Viole Sourdine	8
(in special box)	8			Gedeckt ...	8
Tuba (10-inch				Gemshorn ...	4
wind) ...	8			Zauberflöte ...	4
Octave Coupler				Flautina ...	2
				Clarinet ...	8
				Octave Coupler	
				Swell to Choir	
				3½-inch wind.	

For grandeur of conception, and the amount of variety in tone colour concentrated into its 36 speaking stops, it was epoch-making. It included the first example of modern string tone and the Zauberflöte, or Harmonic Gedeckt. The Great flue-work with its magnificent chorus, conceived and voiced on Schulze-Lewis lines, formed a worthy counterpart to the heavy-pressure reeds, thus anticipating in a remarkable manner the developments of the twentieth-century. The reeds, while lacking the refinement and finish of those which Willis was producing, must have been note-worthy at the time they were voiced. The heavy-pressure 16-ft. reed as the only double in the Swell, and the organ's subsequent removal to Tewkesbury Abbey, have already been mentioned. The complete scheme for its proposed reconstruction will be given later. Another *Multum in Parvo* design, somewhat similar in character, but considerably smaller, is that of St. James's Church, Whitehaven, built by Messrs. Norman & Beard in 1909.

Excluding the Viole Céleste, the scheme comprised but twenty-five speaking registers, the idea being to produce the maximum of variety and effect from the minimum number of stops. Consequently, it was intended to exclude every register which did not contribute in some way or other to the building up of the ensemble. Except for its somewhat truncated Great flue-work, which lacks a compound stop, it can not only provide most of the important effects which can be produced at Tewkesbury, but also many more besides. In its small number of stops are included an independent Pedal reed, heavy-pressure Trombas which play in 8-ft. and 4-ft. pitch on two different manuals, for Tuba effects, a French Trumpet in the Swell and a 16-ft. Clarinet as the double reed. It is possible to play the melody of a Bach Chorale with a prominent 4-ft. reed on the Pedal, and accompany it on the Great flue-work. This frequently cannot be done on instruments more than double the size! Notice also the amount of colour contained in the third manual.

The original scheme read as follows :—

ST. JAMES'S CHURCH, WHITEHAVEN*
(*Norman and Beard*, 1909)

PEDAL ORGAN

ft.

Sub-Bass ⎱ from ⎰ 16
Bass ⎰ Great ⎱
Flute ⎱ 16ft. ⎰ 8
Open Wood ... 16
Octave (18 from
Open Wood)... 8
Trombone ... 16
Orchestral to
Pedal
Great to Pedal
Swell to Pedal
Flue-work :
3½ & 4½-inch wind.
Reed :
8-inch wind.

ORCHESTRAL ORGAN

Quintatön ... 16
Viole d'Orchestre 8
Viole Céleste (to
CC) 8
Hohlflöte (Open
to CC) ... 8
Concert Flute... 4
Octave Coupler
Bombarde to Orchestral
Swell to Orchestral
Wind pressure : 7-inch.

BOMBARDE DIVISION
(Unenclosed) *ft.*

Harmonic ⎱
Tromba ⎰ unit ⎱ 8
Octave ⎰
Tromba ⎰ ⎰ 4
Wind pressure :
7-inch.

GREAT ORGAN

Rohr Bordun ... 16
Claribel Flute
(soft, closed
bass) ... 8
Geigen ... 8
Open Diapason 8
Principal ... 4
Twelfth ... 2⅔
Fifteenth ... 2
Bombarde to Great
Orchestral to Great
Swell to Great
Wind pressure : 3½-inch.

Tubular action throughout. The Swell
soundboard is carried up an extra octave
to complete the effectiveness of the
octave coupler.

SWELL ORGAN

ft.

Horn Diapason 8
Lieblich Gedeckt 8
Geigen Principal 4
Gemshorn ... 2
Mixture 12, 19,
22 III
Corno di Bassetto16
Trumpet (open
Shallots) ... 8
Octave coupler
Octaves alone
Tremulant to
Swell and Or-
chestral
Wind pressure :
7-inch.

---

* As finally carried out the design was altered, to its detriment.
In the Orchestral department an 8-ft. Oboe was substituted for the
Quintatön 16-ft., and the Céleste rank extends only to tenor C. The
Swell contains an Echo Gamba but no separate 2-ft. rank, the Mixture
being 15, 19, 22.

One complete cathedral organ scheme must be given. We cannot do better than choose Willis's historic design for St. Paul's Cathedral of 1872. Its size would now be regarded as moderate, but it served as a model for his numerous cathedral organs for many years. As will be seen, it was at the time revolutionary, and its possibilities were enormous. Nevertheless, comparison with the various departments of the Ely Cathedral organ, already quoted, reveals the immense advances which were made in tonal design, especially as to the Choir and Solo departments, within the next forty years.

The epoch-making Swell has already been alluded to, but notice the fine tonal structure of the Great flue-work, including the now rare Quint $5\frac{1}{3}$-ft. and two compound stops both of which contained the tierce rank, while the Mixture was a high-pitched, repeating Mixture, or Cymbel. The flue-work was topped by three splendid chorus reeds, on heavy wind.

Until Lewis's magnificent example at Southwark, twenty-five years later, no cathedral Great Organ was so well equipped with flue-work and chorus. The effect of the Solo Tubas must have been as electrical as were those at St. George's Hall, Liverpool, six years before. Notice also the tonal structure of the Pedal Organ, with two 32-ft. stops and a Mixture.

St. Paul's Cathedral, London
(*Willis*, 1872)

PEDAL ORGAN

	ft.
Double Open Diapason	32
Open Diapason	16
Violon	16
Octave	8
Violoncello	8
Mixture 17, 19, 22	III
Contra Posaune (light wind)	32
Grand Bombarde (heavy wind)	16
Clarion (heavy wind)	8
Choir to Pedal	
Great to Pedal	
Swell to Pedal	
Solo to Pedal	

CHOIR ORGAN
(Unenclosed)

	ft.
Bourdon	16
Open Diapason	8
Dulciana	8
Violoncello	8
Claribel Flute	8
Lieblich Gedeckt	8
Principal	4
Flûte Harmonique	4
Flageolet	2
Cor Anglais	8
Corno di Bassetto	8

GREAT ORGAN

	ft.
Double Open Diapason	16
Open Diapason (large)	8
Open Diapason (small)	8
Claribel Flute	8
Quint	$5\frac{1}{3}$
Principal	4
Flute Harmonique	4
Octave Quint	$2\frac{2}{3}$
Superoctave	2
Fourniture, 17, 19, 22	III
Mixture, 24, 26, 29	III
Trombone	16
Tromba	8
Clarion	4
Choir to Great	
Swell Suboctave to Great	
Swell to Great	
Swell Octave to Great	
Solo to Great	

WIND PRESSURES
Flue-work :
$2\frac{1}{2}$ to 7-inches.
Reeds :
$3\frac{1}{2}$ to $17\frac{1}{2}$-inches.

SWELL ORGAN
(Stopped Bass)

	ft.
Contra Gamba	16
Open Diapason	8
Lieblich Gedeckt	8
Salicional	8
Vox Angelica (Ten. C)	8
Principal	4
Fifteenth	2
Echo Cornet, 17, 19, 22	III
Contra Posaune	16
Cornopean	8
Hautboy	8
Clarion	4

SOLO ORGAN
(Unenclosed)

	ft.
Flûte Harmonique	8
Concert Flute	4
Corno di Bassetto	8
Orchestral Oboe	8
Tuba Magna	8
Tuba Clarion	4

Finally, as the apotheosis of English tonal design, is given the specification of the organs in Tewkesbury Abbey, now being rebuilt at the time this book goes to press. The famous Norman church has, for many years, possessed two hardly less famous instruments, of which the specification of the larger and more modern has already been given. This was exhibited at South Kensington in 1885 and at Liverpool in 1886. It was purchased by the Rev. C. W. Grove and presented to the Abbey in 1887 to commemorate Queen Victoria's Jubilee. It is now known as the "Grove" organ. The instrument may, without exaggeration, be described as the first really modern British organ, since it anticipated the combination of the bold Schulze-Lewis Diapason chorus with powerful heavy-pressure reeds. The specification was, for its date (1885), a remarkable example of *multum in parvo*, comprising nearly all the essential attributes of a cathedral organ in thirty-five speaking registers. It contained an abundance of variety and tone colour, including the first examples of modern string tone and the earliest specimen in this country of the Zauberflöte or Harmonic Gedeckt.

This instrument was used on special occasions only, and normal services were accompanied on the old "Milton" organ. The latter stands on the south side of the choir and has a superb sixteenth-century case. Much of the pipe-work dates from the seventeenth-century. For a time it belonged to Oliver Cromwell and, according to tradition, it may have been played on by the poet Milton ; hence its name. The old organ finally came to rest at Tewkesbury. It was last restored by Henry Willis in 1848, being one of his first works of any importance. As left by him, it had a Great Organ of thirteen stops, complete with Mixture, Trumpet, and Clarion, but no 16-ft. register. The Swell had six stops, again with no double, and the only reed was an Oboe. The Pedal consisted of Open Wood and Bourdon. The instrument possessed an "old-world" charm to a quite remarkable degree and was, perhaps, the most beautiful pre-1850 organ in the country.

The two instruments are now being rebuilt and combined, but their individual qualities will nevertheless be retained. Both organs were deficient in enclosed accompanimental and mezzo-forte solo effects. This shortcoming will, however, be made good by the addition of a department comprising two manuals and pedal placed in an apsidal chamber, at triforium level, just above the "Milton."

The new section may really be regarded as combining with the rebuilt "Milton" to form a four-manual organ, primarily for accompanimental purposes, since it is of relatively slight power, but has great flexibility. On the north side of the church, opposite to the "Milton," will stand the rebuilt "Grove," somewhat enlarged, but retaining its original tonal characteristics. The most important additions are the expansion of the great tonal structure on a 16-ft. basis and the essential chorus upper-work of the unenclosed Choir Organ. All departments are to be controlled from one very large five-manual stopkey console. The proximity of the two instruments will make it possible for them to be treated as one when desired. In this form they will fulfil every requirement of classical and modern music. The three unenclosed chorus ensembles, with a choice of two independent Pedal Organs, are ideally balanced for rendering the music of Bach and his predecessors with historical accuracy. On the other hand the five well differentiated enclosed manual ensembles are complete, to the point of luxury, for dealing with every kind of modern music. One might perhaps reasonably regret the absence of a large-scaled unenclosed solo Cornet and a heavy 16-ft. reed on the enclosed solo which could have been usefully borrowed on the Pedal.

Nevertheless, Tewkesbury Abbey will possess an instrument tonally more complete than any other in this country. Indeed, it might fairly be claimed that the design, especially having regard to its size, is second to none in the world.

It will be an achievement of which its builders, Messrs. J. W. Walker and Sons Limited, should have every reason to be proud. Moreover, it places Mr. Huskisson Stubington, the Abbey organist, in the front rank of tonal designers.

TEWKESBURY ABBEY (1949)

GROVE PEDAL	ft.
1. Contra Violone ...	32
2. Major Bass	16
3. Violone (20 from No. 1)	16
4. Dolce	16
5. Bourdon (from No. 34)	16
6. Octave	8
7. Major Flute	8
8. Superoctave (20 from No. 6)	4
9. Cornet (12, 15, 17, 19, 22)	V
10. Double Trombone (20 from No. 45) ...	32
11. Bombarde	16
12. Trombone (from No. 45)	16
13. Clarion	8
14. Octave Clarion (20 from No. 13) ...	4
i. Solo to Pedal	
ii. Swell to Pedal	
iii. Great to Pedal	
iv. Choir to Pedal	

MILTON PEDAL	ft.
15. Open Wood	16
16. Bourdon	16
17. Dulciana (from No. 48)	16
18. Bourdon Quint (from No. 16)	10⅔
19. Principal	8
20. Dulciana (from No. 48)	8
21. Flute (20 from No. 16)	8
22. Fifteenth (20 from No. 19)	4
23. Flute	4
24. Trumpet	16
25. Double Hautboy ⎱ from	16
26. Hautboy ⎰ No. 93	8
27. Hautboy	4
v. Swell to Pedal	
vi. Great to Pedal	

ft.

APSE PEDAL (Enclosed)
28. Lieblich Gedeckt (from
    No. 105) 16
29. Lieblich Gedeckt (from
    No. 105) 8
30. Double Horn (from
    No. 115) 32
31. Horn (from No. 115)... 16
    vii. Echo to Pedal
    viii. Solo to Pedal

GROVE GREAT
32. Sub Bourdon (Ten. C)
    (from No. 34)   ... 32
33. Violone   16
34. Bourdon   16
35. Open Diapason I   ... 8
36. Open Diapason II   ... 8
37. Claribel   8
38. Quint 5⅓
39. Octave   4
40. Geigen Principal   ... 4
41. Tierce 3⅕
42. Septième   ...   ... 2²⁄₇
43. Rauschquinte (12, 15) II
44. Mixture (19, 22, 26, 29) IV
45. Trombone   16
46. Tromba   8
47. Clarion   4
    ix. Solo to Great
    x. Swell to Great
    xi. Choir to Great

ft.

MILTON GREAT
48. Double Dulciana   ... 16
49. Open Diapason I   ... 8
50. Open Diapason II   ... 8
51. Stopped Diapason   ... 8
52. Clarabelle   8
53. Principal   4
54. Flute Harmonique   ... 4
55. Twelfth 2⅔
56. Fifteenth   2
57. Tierce 1⅗
58. Fourniture (19, 22, 26) III
59. Trumpet   8
60. Clarion   4
61. Cremona (Ten. C)   ... 8
62. Hautboy (Swell)   ... 8
    xii. Echo to Great
    xiii. Apse Solo to Great
    xiv. Swell to Great

GROVE CHOIR
63. Bourdon (from No. 34) 16
64. Spitzflöte   8
65. Gedeckt   8
66. Viole Sourdine   ... 8
67. Gemshorn   4
68. Zauberflöte 4
69. Flautino   2
70. Larigot 1⅓
71. Octavin   1
72. Scharf (26, 29, 33) ... III
73. Clarinet   8
    xv. Milton Great on Choir
    xvi. Echo to Choir
    xvii. Grove Solo to Choir
    xviii. Swell to Choir

GROVE SWELL		ft.
74.	Open Diapason ...	8
75.	Flauto Traverso ...	8
76.	Viol di Gamba ...	8
77.	Voix Célestes (Ten. C)	8
78.	Geigen	4
79.	Fifteenth	2
80.	Mixture (12, 19, 22) ...III	
81.	Sharp Mixture (26, 29) II	
82.	Contra Posaune ...	16
83.	Trumpet	8
84.	Oboe	8
85.	Clarion	4
xix.	Tremulant	
xx.	Octave	
xxi.	Suboctave	
xxii.	Solo to Swell	

MILTON SWELL		
86.	Open Diapason ...	8
87.	Flute à Cheminée ...	8
88.	Salicional	8
89.	Vox Angelica (Ten. C)	8
90.	Principal	4
91.	Flute	4
92.	Mixture (15, 19, 22) ...III	
93.	Double Hautboy ...	16
94.	Echo Trumpet ...	8
95.	Hautboy ⎫ 49 ⎧	8
96.	Octave ⎬ from ⎨	8
	Hautboy ⎭ No. 93 ⎩	4
xxiii.	Tremulant	
xxiv.	Octave	
xxv.	Suboctave	
xxvi.	Echo to Swell	
xxvii.	Apse Solo to Swell	

GROVE SOLO		ft.
(Enclosed except No. 104)		
97.	Contra viola ...	16
98.	Violoncello	8
99.	Violoncello Vibrato	8
	(Ten. C)	
100.	Violetta	4
101.	Concert Flute ...	4
102.	Cornetto di Viole	
	(10, 12, 15) ...III	
103.	Orchestral Trumpet	8
104.	Tuba	8
xxviii.	Octave	
xxix.	Suboctave	
xxx.	Great to Solo	

APSE SOLO (Enclosed)		
105.	Lieblich Gedeckt ...	16
106.	Harmonic Flute ...	8
107.	Aeoline	8
108.	Flute Octaviante ...	4
109.	Nazard	2⅔
110.	Piccolo	2
111.	Tierce	1⅗
112.	Septième	1⅐
113.	Corno di Bassetto ...	8
114.	Orchestral Oboe ...	8
115.	Double Horn ...	16
116.	Horn (49 from No.	
	115)	8
xxxi.	Tremulant	
xxxii.	Octave	
xxxiii.	Suboctave	

APSE ECHO (Enclosed)

117.	Quintatön	...	16
118.	Dolce	...	8
119.	Unda Maris (Ten. C)		8
120.	Cor de Nuit	...	8
121.	Dolcissimo	...	4
122.	Flauto Amabile	...	4
123.	Harmonica Aetheria (12, 15)	...	II
124.	Voix Humaine	...	8
xxxiv.	Tremulant		
xxxv.	Octave		
xxxvi.	Suboctave		
xxxvii.	Independent pedal		
xxxviii.	Double touch canceller		
xxxix.	Gt. and Ped. combs. off (Grove)		
xl.	Gt. and Ped. combs. off (Milton)		
xli.	Milton Great chorus reeds on Swell		

53 thumb pistons
3 general cancel pistons
3 control pistons
  and a variety of other accessories
Electric action
Three Discus blowers
165 stop keys

WIND PRESSURES :

Milton Organ

Great :	Flues	...	3¾ inches
	Reeds	...	6 inches
Swell :	All	...	4½ inches
Pedal :	Flues	...	4½ inches
	Reed	...	6 inches

Apse Organ

Echo and Solo	...	4 inches
Reed	...	6 inches

Grove Organ

Great :	Flues	...	4½ inches	Solo :	Flues	...	6 inches
	Reeds	...	8 inches		Reeds	...	16 inches
Swell :	Flues	...	5 inches	Pedal :	Flues	...	5 inches
	Reeds	...	8 inches		Reeds	...	16 inches
Choir :	All	...	4 inches				

The Extension Organ

Something must now be said about " Extension." The particular case of " borrowing " in octave, suboctave, and other pitches is its oldest form, and in modern times has come to be called " extension." The principle has been used on the Pedal Organ in this country for nearly a century ; it was extensively employed by Schulze at Doncaster in 1862. It was strongly advocated by Hopkins and has been used by English builders ever since. It is now almost universally accepted.

Its use on the manuals, however, which was also advocated by Schulze, gave rise to much controversy. It has been supported with such doubtful arguments by its friends, and attacked on such false grounds by its enemies, that it is difficult to consider it dispassionately.

In its essence, it is simply the coupling in octave, sub-octave, and other pitches, of selected single ranks of pipes of complete compass. It is not a little remarkable that the most strenuous opponents among organ-builders do not scruple to fill their instruments with a copious array of octave and suboctave couplers. Many players also do not hesitate to use these indiscriminately, thus producing a much more ill-balanced effect than even a badly designed extension instrument. One advantage of an extension organ is that octave and suboctave couplers, as separate draw-knobs or stop-keys, are almost entirely absent ; consequently, abuse is impossible. Their appropriate selective use, with suitable ranks, is inherent in the instrument itself but (provided it is properly designed) the balance is not upset.

In the ordinary organ, each stop-knob controls at least

one rank of pipes. In the extension instrument, one rank furnishes material for several stop-knobs. Indeed, extension is not economical unless a set of pipes can do duty for at least three pitches. For instance, a rank of 97 Salicional pipes can be arranged to produce six stops, 16-ft,, 8-ft., 4-ft., $2\frac{2}{3}$-ft., 2-ft. and Mixture II (19, 22). The unit might quite well appear on the Pedal in one or two pitches, and on another manual as well. To do this in the ordinary organ would require some hundreds of pipes. But if indiscriminately employed, extension undoubtedly produces an unbalanced effect, and there is a likelihood that one note, when played, will be much less powerful than another, because a number of its pipes may already be sounding at the behest of another note. But this drawback is slight, compared with the chaos produced by indiscriminate octave and suboctave coupling in the ordinary organ. In small organs, extension is less satisfactory owing to the want of variety in tone that the necessarily restricted number of ranks supplies, and the difficulty of building up a properly balanced chorus. Judicious extension may well be used in augmenting the resources by adding certain units, as in the reconstruction of the organ at Holy Trinity Church, Hull. One great advantage of the extension organ is its compactness, which is of importance where, as is often the case, space in churches is limited. A characteristic specimen of a thorough-going extension organ is that at the B.B.C. Studio, Maida Vale, London, well known to wireless listeners. This instrument was originally intended for accompanimental purposes only, and this, coupled with restricted space and other considerations, justified Messrs. Compton in exploiting extension to a much greater extent than they would ordinarily have considered desirable. But so successfully did they carry out their economical scheme that the organ has been used for recital purposes with considerable success, having won for itself an enviable reputation. It has three manuals and upwards of fifty speaking stops derived from only eleven extension units, enclosed in two swell boxes. The total number of pipes is approximately 1,100. Noteworthy is the Cornet unit, comprising 340 open pipes, which furnishes Cornets sounding the harmonics of 32-ft., 16-ft., and 8-ft., respectively. Their effectiveness has already been described in Chapter 1. But at its best, extension is not carried to such extremes, and it is desirable that, wherever possible, the primary flue and reed choruses should be unextended, and this is what Messrs. Compton themselves prefer. In particular, they like to avoid simultaneous use on one manual of one rank at adjacent pitches, such as 16-ft. and 8-ft., or 8-ft. and 4-ft. The primary flue chorus should generally be unenclosed. We will now give an example of the judicious use of extension in a fairly large three-manual organ, possessing twenty-six units. Messrs. Compton have kindly supplied the following chart, clearly showing the extension scheme of their fine organ at St. Luke's Church, Chelsea, London. The name of the ranks appears on the left, and the pitches at which they appear on the different claviers is shown in the remaining columns.

ST. LUKE'S CHURCH, CHELSEA, LONDON
(*John Compton Organ Co.*, 1933)

	Chamber 1	ft.	Pedal	Great	Choir	Bombard	Swell
1	Open Wood	16	32.16.8.4	—	—	—	—
2	Open Metal	16	16	—	—	—	—
3	Sub-Bass ...	32	32.16.8.4	—	—	—	—
4	Diapason I	8	—	8	—	8	—
5	Diapason II	16	—	16.4	8	4	—
6	Diapason III	8	—	8.2	4	—	—
7	Violone ...	16	16.8	16.8	8	—	—
8	Salicional I	16	16	8.2⅔.2	16.4.1⅓.1	—	—
9	Salicional II	4	—	4	8.2⅔.2	—	—
10	Vox Angelica, 2 ranks	8	—	—	8.4	—	—
11	Harmonic Flute ...	8	—	8	—	—	—
12	Stopped Diapason ..	16	—	16.8.5⅓.4	8.4.2⅔.2	—	—
13	Diaphonic Horn ...	16	16	8	—	16.8	—
14	Trombone	16	16.8	8	—	8.4	—
15	Posaune I	32	32.16	8	—	16	—
16	Posaune II	8	—	16.4	—	8	—
17	Clarinet ...	16	16	—	16.8	—	—
	Chamber 2						
18	Geigen I ...	8	—	—	—	—	8
19	Geigen II...	4	—	—	—	—	4
20	Viola da Gamba ...	16	—	—	—	—	16.8.4.2⅔.2
21	Viole Céleste	4	—	—	—	—	8(T.C.).4
22	Rohr Gedeckt	16	16.8	—	—	—	16.8.4.2
23	Trumpet I	16	16	—	—	16.4	8
24	Trumpet II	4	—	—	—	8	4
25	Oboe ...	16	16.8	—	—	—	16.8.4
26	Orchestral Hautboy	16	16	—	—	—	16.8

In addition, there are Mixtures as follows, whose derivation is too complicated to be shown in the table :—

Pedal :	Fourniture	15, 19, 22, 26, 29	5 ranks
Bombarde :	Fourniture	12, 15, 19, 22, 26, 29	6 ranks
Great :	Plein Jeu	19, 22, 26, 29	4 ranks increasing to 8 in treble
	Petite Cymbale	26, 29, 33, 36	4 ranks
Swell :	Cymbale	22, 26, 29	3 ranks

In extension Mixtures, the quints are, of course, tempered. Though slightly out of tune, the defect is hardly more noticeable than in the ordinary Mixture, unless it has been freshly tuned.

It will be seen that the Great Organ flue chorus can be built up almost entirely from unextended material, and the same applies to the reeds, the 8-ft. being independent, while the 16-ft. and 4-ft. reeds come from one unit. This is also true of the Salicional foundation of the Choir Organ, one Salicional rank supplying the 16-ft., 4-ft., 1⅓-ft. and 1-ft. stops, while the second supplies the 8-ft., 2⅔-ft. and 2-ft. stops. If the scheme has a serious shortcoming, it is the lack of a tierce rank in any part of the instrument. Its total enclosure is also to be regretted.

It cannot be over-stressed that extension needs most careful and experienced handling, both tonally and mechanically. If lightheartedly embarked upon, the results in both respects may well be disastrous.

*   *   *   *

From what has been written, and from the examples given, those who are interested should have gleaned some ideas as to how to draw up an effective and resourceful specification. In these days when economy is so vital, the problem will nearly always be that of getting the best effect from a limited number of stops. To this end, it will be necessary carefully to consider the introduction of each and every register, not so much from the point of view of its beauty, or even of its general utility, still less of personal preference, but how far it will fit into the design as a whole, and to what extent it will contribute to the building up of a complete ensemble. The insertion of soft 8-ft. stops which add nothing to the general effect must be reduced to an absolute minimum. They may, however, be used occasionally in small designs as manual doubles to tenor C, when they add quite appreciably to the ensemble effect. A Salicional in 16-ft. pitch can be heard distinctly, even with the box closed, when added to an unenclosed Tuba, though the former is the softest and the latter the loudest stop in the organ. In 8-ft. pitch, however, it would make little, if any, addition, even to a light combination.

Players, especially of large instruments, naturally tend to include just those stops which they like best, or find most useful, quite regardless of the design as a whole. The result is that a small organ is too often simply a chunk out of a large one, instead of being, as it ought to be, an entity of its own, complete as far as may be ; that is, a larger instrument in miniature. Remember that the Great is the most important department, and if it has but half-a-dozen stops it should comprise a double (even if only to tenor C) and a chorus complete at any rate to the Fifteenth. The 4-ft. Flute is by no means indispensable. In the Swell, the 16-ft. reed is the foundation, and a Mixture and 8-ft. chorus reed should be included. The 8-ft. Oboe can quite well be done without. The third manual can either be an unenclosed miniature Great, or a more highly coloured enclosed department, but it should never be inserted before the Great, Swell and, especially, the Pedal are reasonably complete. If there is an independent open 16-ft. on the Pedal, the soft stops can quite well be supplied by borrowing manual doubles. The importance of the independent Pedal 16-ft. reed cannot be over-emphasised. It should precede and not follow the unenclosed manual 8-ft. reed and the third manual, though it can usefully be extended to form manual reeds of 8-ft. and 4-ft. pitches. These should be made playable from another manual, apart from the Great Organ. One or two 8-ft. and 4-ft. Pedal stops should be included wherever possible.

With regard to mechanism, where the wind pressure does not exceed $3\frac{1}{2}$ inches, and where there are not more than half-a-dozen stops on each manual, tracker action is all that is necessary or desirable, but even in small organs, pneumatic action must be used for the pedals. In larger instruments, electric action will be used throughout.

These few remarks may be found helpful, but much more can be learnt about tonal design from the study of the numerous illustrations which have been given. A thorough understanding of the appropriate registration of organ music of every period and style is also of vital importance. The studies of tonal design and registration are, indeed, almost inseparable.

Chapter IV

REGISTRATION

The development of the tonal structure of the British organ during the last hundred years has been gone into at some length. It is now proposed to consider how the player can get the finest effects from a modern instrument. It must be borne in mind, however, that what follows refers to British, rather than Continental, players and instruments.

A great deal about organ registration has been written from time to time, but nearly all by players for the guidance of other players. What the ordinary musical listener actually hears at a distance from the instrument, where the majority sit, or, more important still, what he does not hear, has hardly been considered. After all, it is he who really matters most, and if it is not possible for him to appreciate what is going on, the player labours but in vain. However satisfactory certain combinations or methods of playing sound at the keys or close to the organ, if these cannot be clearly appreciated by the listeners at a distance, it is wasted effort.

The great trouble with a big organ as generally played, when heard at a distance, is its want of clearness, especially if the building be at all resonant. Let us glance at the orchestra for a moment, where we find that the clearest results are obtained from the small number of instruments as used, say, by Mozart. To follow the score of the G minor Symphony, well-conducted and skilfully played by an orchestra of suitable size, is a sheer delight, as every point comes out. Can the same be said when one listens, with the music, to Bach's great Prelude and Fugue in A minor, for example, as usually rendered by our finest players on a large modern organ? Consider, again, that most perfect combination on which some of our greatest composers have expressed their inmost thoughts—the string quartet. Nothing can approach it for clearness of detail, least of all the organ as it is commonly heard. It is not for one moment suggested that organ players should attempt to imitate the tone colours of the orchestra or string quartet. But that is no reason why, in registration and general rendering, the characteristics of the Mozart orchestra and the string quartet should not be borne in mind. Players can make many useful experiments by getting some musical friend, who need not be an organ expert, to hear the effects they are producing in the church (or other building) at a considerable distance, as they are heard by the majority of listeners. This is what was done at St. Bees, where the church is slightly resonant when empty— just enough to take off the sharp edges. Some interesting and important discoveries will be made.*

It will be found, for instance, that the finer shades of tone, apparent enough to the player near the organ, are altogether lost in the distance. Contrasts in the quality of registers must be much greater, and tone-colouring more vivid than may appear desirable at close quarters. This is particularly true of trio playing : to be really effective, the widest possible contrasts in tone should be chosen. An example of the opposite kind may be given. Some French

* It is not a little remarkable that Mr. Reginald Whitworth, the well-known authority, should have anticipated, quite independently, some of the most salient features of this chapter. About 1937, he enumerated these in his unpublished " Notes on Registration," which were compiled some years before the present writers had the privilege of his intimate personal friendship.

composers direct the use of the 8-ft. and 4-ft. Gedeckts on one manual contrasted with 8-ft. and 4-ft. open Flutes on another. This may sound satisfactory to the player, but the difference is almost inappreciable at a distance. Much greater contrast is necessary. Many of the subtleties suggested by Karg-Elert are quite lost on the listener, however they may sound to the player, assuming they are practicable. Detailed registration directions given by composers and editors are often better ignored. Careful experiments should be made to discover what is most effective on any one particular organ, and, more important still, in the building itself. Again, it will be found that the instrument appears far less brilliant in the distance. Combinations which seem top heavy at the keys will appear properly balanced. The reason for this is that acute sounds are readily absorbed in a spacious building. It is well known that manual basses and pedal notes travel much better than those of high pitch. Even more important, it will be discovered that a considerable number of smaller 8-ft. and 4-ft. stops usually included in bigger combinations are not only superfluous, as they make no material addition, but are positively harmful, as they tend to destroy that clearness in effect which is essential, especially in contrapuntal music. The player may be surprised to find that, in such combinations, the smaller 8-ft. stops can all be dispensed with, as well as the 4-ft. Flutes.

In the full Great, for instance, with finely-voiced chorus reeds, one representative of each pitch in the Diapason family will generally be sufficient, and the gain in clearness of effect will be very marked. If a good Clarion is present, the Principal may even be dispensed with. It will also be found that the tone is steadier, and the instrument will sound better in tune than is usually the case. At St. Bees, no manual combination in the organ, except the full Great (which includes the Open Diapason and the Tromba), is set to draw more than one 8-ft. stop. A well-appointed full Great ought to be self-sufficient. The usual addition of the full Swell is generally detrimental. Not only is the increase in power unimportant, but the two sets of chorus reeds tend to fight, as they are hardly ever dead in tune, so the purity of effect is spoilt. Many players never seem to build up their Great separately, without the Swell coupled. In some instances, this is unfortunately due to its being subordinate to the Swell, which has more than its proper share of the good things : these ought to belong to the more important department. Where the tonal structure of the Great flue-work is reasonably complete, it can be most effectively built up without the assistance of the Swell.

The continuous use of the Swell to Great coupler leads to lazy methods of registration. It is much easier to obtain an increase of power by opening the Swell box than by adding stops to the Great Organ. Consequently, we get a surfeit of the stereotyped " Great Diapasons with Swell reeds coupled " which is so monotonous. When crescendos from the Swell organ are really necessary, a much finer effect is obtained by coupling the Swell double reed and Mixture work, omitting the 8 and 4-ft. reeds. Such a combination will also be less likely to be out of tune with the Great. When the Swell chorus reeds are drawn, the box should not remain open except for very short periods. It must be remembered that, while fine reed tone can be very impressive and even thrilling, it is fatiguing to the ear and soon palls on the listener. If a continuous forte is required, the Great flue chorus work should be used without the Swell reeds. If more power still is necessary, a better effect is obtained by discreet employment of the Great reeds. It should be remembered that the constant coupling of the Swell to the Great virtually reduces these two manuals to one, with a corresponding loss of variety and contrast, especially when passages on each are required to be played alternately.

The elimination of superfluous stops also improves lesser combinations such as full to Fifteenth or Mixture, and on the Great the addition of reed tone spoils the characteristic effect of either. Similar principles apply even to still smaller combinations. It is not only unnecessary, but also undesirable, to use the 4-ft. Flute with the Principal. The combination of 8-ft. Flutes with Diapasons, beloved by most players is a common example of one tone spoiling the other. How much greater would be the variety, and better the effect, if they were kept separate, and only very occasionally combined ! The habitual use of the Stopped Diapason with the 8-ft. open Flute is another example of the same evil, whereby the characteristic quality of each is spoilt. The principles here enunciated are applicable to quite small organs. The staple fare with some players for *mf* effects, whether appropriate or not, often seems to consist of all the Great Diapasons and Flutes, plus the Swell reeds, with most of the Pedal fluework—a nondescript, neutral tint combination of a deadly dull character. An effect equally impressive, but much cleaner and steadier in tone, can, in most cases, be produced, when desirable, with two manual stops, the double and large open only, backed by the Pedal Open Wood and the 32-ft. This so-called " rolling effect " ought not to be regarded as a stock combination, but should be reserved for sostenuto passages of a grave and solemn character. Its impressiveness is enhanced by infrequent use. With adjustable pistons, it may be effectively contrasted with a lighter combination, such as the small Open Diapason and some upper-work. The over-employment of heavy Diapason combinations has a depressing effect upon listeners, and tends to get the organ into disrepute with musicians generally. There are reasons of a different kind for the improved effect of sparse registrations. Owing to changes of temperature, an organ does not remain in perfect tune for more than a short time, and it is seldom that slight robbing and unsteadiness in the wind supply do not occur. Apart from losses due to sympathy, it follows that, the smaller the number of stops in use at any one time, the less chance there is of these disturbing causes operating and the steadier will be the result. In such combinations as full to Fifteenth or Mixture, or, *a fortiori*, when two or three heavy-pressure reeds are added, is there any reason whatever why every 8-ft. and 4-ft. flue stop should also be drawn ? To secure the best effect in building up combinations of increasing power, the process should be selective rather than cumulative. In other words, it may be found better to subtract some stops when others are added. For instance, in a number of instruments, the large Open Diapason is too big, and is best withdrawn from most flue-work combinations. With modern adjustables there should be no difficulty in arranging this.

In his valuable book, " The Organ," the late Sir Percy Buck points out that, as with the orchestra, there are many ways of playing *forte*, and he mentions a few. " Most players," he adds, " seem to know only one ; full to Fifteenth with full Swell coupled." It is desirable, for the sake of variety, to get away occasionally from the stereotyped full Great, full to Mixture, or even full to Fifteenth. In building up to the full Great, it is usual to add the 8-ft. reed (often before the

Mixtures), then the 16-ft., if present, and lastly the Clarion. As a rule it is better to begin with the 16-ft. and end with the 4-ft., but occasionally this order may be reversed with advantage. For a change, the 8-ft. reed may be omitted from the full. If the quality be first class, full reeds alone is very impressive, especially in French music. On the other hand, full Great to Mixtures alone, without any reeds, is a characteristic effect which belongs to the organ exclusively. It has no counterpart in the orchestra or any other instrument. It is most valuable in accompanying congregational singing. A particularly thrilling effect can be produced by playing the melody on the full Pedal with reed and the solo Tuba coupled, against an accompaniment on the full Great to Mixture without reeds. This method is recommended by the late Mr. H. Heathcote Statham in his book " The Organ and its Position in Musical Art," which will be referred to later. It was also anticipated by Dom Bédos. A grand effect in sostenuto passages can be produced by substituting the manual 16-ft. reed for the flue double in the full to Mixture. Many unusual combinations in flue-work can be tried, but they will, of course, vary with the type of instrument, and some of these suggestions may be found to be inapplicable. Where a thinner effect is desired, the Twelfth may be omitted from the full to Fifteenth or, conversely, the Twelfth may be used without the Fifteenth. The double may be withdrawn from the full to Fifteenth or Mixture with advantage in contrapuntal music. Unusual combinations such as double open, 8-ft. reed, Principal and Mixture may be tried. A variant would be : double, 8-ft. Flute, Principal or even Clarion. Alternatively the 8-ft. might be omitted. A still more unusual combination, but worth trying, would be : Flutes surmounted by Twelfth, Fifteenth, and even Mixture. Such effects as these should be used with discretion, but a player who can exercise his ingenuity would doubtless discover others more appropriate to his own particular instrument. The Stopped Diapason or even the 8-ft. Flute, with the Twelfth, played solo in the tenor register, sometimes affords a passable imitation of a big Clarinet.

The finest effects of any organ, especially a small instrument, cannot be successfully exploited without much hand registration. Pistons and composition pedals are useful servants, but hard taskmasters, especially if their combinations cannot be easily changed. Reliance on piston pushing is responsible for much dull playing, particularly on larger instruments. In the recommendations made here, hand registration must often be resorted to, though easily adjustable combinations will be of some assistance.

The guiding principle of using no more stops than are necessary to obtain the result aimed at, when heard at a distance, and of ruthlessly eliminating every register which makes no material addition so far as the listener is concerned, applies even more forcibly to the full Swell. Just as the Diapason and its chorus are the foundation of the Great, so a complete family of fine chorus reeds is the true foundation of the modern English Swell—first adumbrated by Willis at St. Paul's in 1872. If these be present, they, together with the Fifteenth and Mixture only, will often produce the most satisfactory result. The classical example is to be found at St. Bees. The Contra Posaune, Cornopean and Clarion on 7-inch wind are magnificent specimens; though voiced as long ago as 1898, they may have been equalled, but never surpassed. The pistons are all adjustable, and this five-stop full Swell was set when the organ was finished in 1899. All the other combinations have been changed frequently, but this one has never been altered, because it cannot be improved.

Strangers have been deceived, and were only convinced, after going up to the console, that but five speaking stops were in use, and the Swell has no couplers. In some full Swells, even the 8-ft. reed may be omitted with advantage, and this is a useful variant. It is generally recognised that the two most essential stops in the full Swell are the 16-ft. reed and the Mixture. If either of these be absent, the effect is incomplete. If they are both first-class specimens, a small full Swell is sometimes possible with these two stops alone, to which the octave coupler may be added, should one be available. This can sometimes be simulated on the ordinary light-pressure organ with the conventional Swell by using the Fifteenth, Mixture and 8-ft. chorus reed with the octave and suboctave couplers. If the bottom and top octaves are avoided the result is passable, and much superior to the muddy effect of the orthodox full Swell, including every stop from Bourdon to the usual pair of 8-ft. reeds. Again, to quote Sir Percy Buck (*op. cit.*): " Sparingly used, the full Swell produces a fine effect, but it is much over-used. It might almost be said that the ability and musicianship of an organist are in inverse proportion to his use of the swell pedal." Many years ago, Thomas Casson pointed out that, thrilling though the modern full Swell undoubtedly is, its dynamic crescendo is no more a real one, acoustically, than that of a brass band approaching round a corner. It is certainly far from being true expression, because the box smothers the foundation even more than the over-tones.

With regard to the smaller flue combinations, the same principles apply as on the Great, and an intelligent listener at a distance will supply much valuable help. Speaking generally, it will be found that a combination of registers of different pitches is more effective than if they were of the same pitch. If an increase of power be desired, it will be found much better to add some of the upper work (which is acoustically correct) than to multiply the number of 8-ft. stops. A single stop of given power sounds much more satisfactory than two or more soft ones of the same pitch. As Sir Percy Buck so well says (*op. cit.*) : "Never use two stops where one will do."

The late Sir Walter Parratt's plea for single 8-ft. stops (and uncoupled manuals) is even more valid now, having regard to the greater variety of tonal resources in the modern organ.* The Oboe, for instance, like the Great 8-ft. and 4-ft. Flutes, is much overworked in combination, and, if a first-class reed, is far more effective alone. It makes no addition to the 8-ft. chorus reed or full Swell unless it be out of tune, which it generally is, and its characteristic quality is needlessly obscured by the addition of flue-work. The late Dr. A. Eaglefield Hull, in his excellent book on "Organ Playing," says : "There is no stop on the organ which present custom so badly abuses." Quite frequently one sees the following combination of four stops (all 8-ft.) suggested : Violin Diapason, Lieblich Gedeckt, Echo Gamba and Oboe. The various stops effectually kill each other, and simply serve to produce a "mash" of tone. But there is a high authority for this : one of the Swell pistons on the R.C.O. organ is actually set to draw a similar combination of *four* 8-ft. stops ! Speaking generally, a neutral tint of this kind tends to that dullness and monotony of which musicians who are not organists so properly complain.

Again, first-class modern reed stops sound most effective

---

* In this connection, Dr. H. G. Ley's weighty words may be quoted : " The truest economy [in registration] is that which considers the individuality of a stop first of all, and he who makes music out of little is the greater artist."

when used by themselves, without any flue-work of the same pitch. For instance, there is no need to add a Stopped Diapason or 8-ft. Flute to a good Clarinet, or an Open Diapason to a Tromba. Well-voiced reeds, properly finished, ought not to require flue-work to bolster them up or to hide their defects. Flue-work of higher pitch, however, can often be so used. A good 16-ft. reed will go well with flue chorus above it. A 4-ft. Flute, or even a Piccolo, can be used with the Clarinet. The latter combination, in the tenor register, sometimes supplies a passable imitation of the Cor Anglais. Flue stops of widely different timbre, such as the Flute and the Viol, can occasionally be used together.

The principles enunciated can be applied with advantage to combinations on the Choir Organ. If it be enclosed, care should be taken to let the box remain open for ordinary use, and only to close it for special purposes. The effect of this department is lost on the listener if it be treated as an echo Swell. While it may also have accompanimental and solo obligations, its real function is that of a miniature Great Organ. Choir Organs originally voiced for the open have frequently been ruined by enclosure, especially in large buildings. Where the unenclosed Choir has an effective set of modern Mutations their use for solo and other purposes on their own manual is obvious. Many fine effects can also be produced by coupling them in unison, suboctave or octave pitch to the light flue-work of the Great.

A few words about the most effective use of solo stops may not be out of place. Here again, though passages on the woodwind of the orchestra come out well as a rule, they are ineffective as usually heard on the organ. In using such stops, care should be taken to make them much more prominent than may appear necessary at close quarters.

Registers such as the Orchestral Hautboy and Cor Anglais, like the Violes, are penetrating in tone but do not travel well. The same is true to a lesser extent of the Clarinet and Bassoon, and solo passages on some of these stops may be altogether lost to the listeners. As with the Choir, the safest plan is to keep the box open, and only to close it when required for special effects. This applies even more forcibly to solos on the Swell Oboe. Whatever may have been the drawbacks of the old unenclosed Solo Organ, the orchestral registers were at any rate always distinctly heard. Solo passages in the orchestra do not as a rule die away into nothingness, as so frequently happens with their organ counterparts when the box closes. In a first-class modern instrument, highly finished chorus reeds make effective solo stops. Few players seem to take advantage of them, but give us a profusion of Flute solos, which, however beautiful, are much less interesting. Reed solos are often more strikingly effective in the middle or tenor registers, while Flutes are more telling in the upper part of their compass. A good Open Diapason or Geigen used in this way is not to be despised. At the other end of the scale such soft stops as the Salicional and Echo Viol are most restful, but why are they so rarely heard without the Angelica or Célestes ? The employment of these fancy registers in pianissimo passages should surely be the exception and not the rule ; sparing use serves to heighten their effect. After all, they are simply out of tune ranks—" a gross libel " as someone said " on the harmony of the spheres." In larger buildings these extremely soft effects are often overdone. The orchestral pianissimo can always be easily heard, and is quite distinct.

With regard to the accompaniments of solo stops, the wider the contrast the more effective they will sound. If this is well marked, they need not be too soft. Flutes should not, of course, be used to accompany a solo Flute, and reeds to accompany another reed. Gambas and soft reeds form the best accompaniment for a solo Flute, and soft Flutes for Violes or light reeds. The conventional Dulciana accompaniment for the Oboe is too indistinct to be properly heard, and too near it in tone quality to be effective. The Cornopean is best accompanied by the Great Flute or Stopped Diapason and the Tromba by the Swell flue-work with the box open. The most effective accompaniment to the Solo Tuba is the Great flue-work, say, to Fifteenth or Mixture alone. If, as is usually the case, the full Swell be coupled, not only is the characteristic effect of the Great flue-work spoilt, but the thrill that is produced by the entire contrast of the pure flue-work against the big solo reed is lost.

On the Pedal Organ, the principle of using the fewest possible registers to obtain the required effect is still more important, especially when, as is sometimes the case, the wind supply is insufficient. For example, while the Open Wood is drawn such stops as Sub-Bass, Dulciana, Salicional, Bass Flute, and even the milder Violone make but little difference to the general effect, and only consume wind. The real Violone or Contra Bass adds perceptibly, and so does the Open Diapason metal unless it be quite small. The constant use of 16-ft. tone should be avoided. Some players appear to be under the impression that they will be considered incompetent unless they are pedalling continuously with 16-ft. stops. But look at any orchestral score and observe how often the 'cellos play without the double basses. In a very small instrument with only a Sub-Bass, this may be shut in, and use made of the Pedal couplers alone. On the other hand—as Stainer long ago pointed out—most impressive effects can be produced by a heavy pedal with 32-ft. entering after a considerable period of silence, especially when heard under the surge of a fine full Swell. Incidentally, Stainer also used to remark that he generally tried to arrange for each stop in the (Willis, 1872) organ at St. Paul's to be heard at some time or other during the service (including, of course, the Voluntary)—even the Tuba. This might well be taken to heart by many players. One too frequently attends services at churches (and cathedrals also) known to possess fine organs, only to come away disappointed at the colourless and ineffective playing. Except for the full Swell and possibly the 32-ft. open, one might just as well be listening to an ordinary two-manual containing about a dozen registers. It is not for one moment suggested that more stops should be used, or that the absolute power should be materially increased in the quieter parts of the service. It is, however, recommended that, from the listener's point of view, more variety, colour, and brightness might be imparted, instead of the deadly dull accompaniments one too often hears. The exclusive employment of 8-ft. stops on the manuals and 16-ft. tone on the Pedal, has a depressing effect on singers as well as listeners. In the congregational hymn, where, as a rule, the choir need not be considered, restraint is not so important. Then, the heavier reeds or full to Mixture with a big Pedal can be used with thrilling effect. This undoubtedly inspires the congregation to sing more heartily.

Those who are fortunate in having a good specimen of an open 32-ft. should remember that its effect is more telling when used in moderation. In the full Pedal, the only essentials are the 32-ft., the Open Wood 16-ft. and 8-ft., the reeds, and, of course, the upper work, if available. A first-class Pedal 16-ft. reed, like its manual counterpart, can effectively be used alone or with the addition of the Octave Wood 8-ft. or other upper work for solo purposes. Obviously, a pungent

Violone or Contra Bass can be used similarly for smaller solo effects, likewise the Great or Swell double reeds if they are good, through the appropriate Pedal coupler.

Let us now consider how the use, and frequently the abuse, of couplers strikes the musical listener. Sir Walter Parratt was wont to tell his pupils that " the Swell to Great was the first stop the ordinary organist draws and the last he puts in." Nowadays, with electric or pneumatic action in all but quite small organs, he might have omitted " ordinary," for nearly everybody does it—even cathedral organists. But why ? A modern organ has always a reversible piston or pedal for this coupler, so there is certainly no need for it to be constantly drawn. The freshness and beauty of an uncoupled Great has only to be heard to be appreciated, yet how seldom is the listener allowed that pleasure. Full to Mixture alone is *the* organ *par excellence*, but how often can it be heard ? It is an effect which has absolutely no equivalent in the orchestra. Composers and arrangers are not entirely free from blame ; sometimes one sees " full to Fifteenth with full Swell coupled " directed and never a crescendo indicated. Fine flue-work is thus needlessly spoilt by the reedy Swell background, often out of tune. Organ players, who would not tolerate such choral singing or (should they be conductors) their orchestras playing out of tune, appear not to trouble to avoid those combinations which happen to be offenders in this respect ; but that need not be so. It is recorded that Schulze (but he was no lover of the Swell) used to leave the church when the rising temperature put the Swell out of tune with the Great. Many crescendos and diminuendos marked are unnecessary. On the "Willis"-type of instrument with increasingly brilliant trebles (acoustically correct) most of the shorter crescendos and diminuendos, which naturally occur in rising and falling passages, are inherent in the Great Organ itself, without any assistance from the Swell. Another point, when alternate passages are directed to be played on Great and Swell, the contrast is heightened if they are uncoupled. Similar observations apply to the use of the Swell-to-Choir, though there is more excuse for it, as our Choir Organs are usually such puny things. The Solo-to-Great also is much over-used. A well-appointed full Great with heavy pressure chorus reeds is amply sufficient for all but the most exceptional climaxes, and is certainly enough for ordinary fortissimo endings. It should not be forgotten that the Tuba is a solo stop, and ought not to be treated as a super chorus reed, save on rare occasions. In French music, where fortissimo chords occur high in the compass, the Tuba in suboctave pitch may occasionally be coupled to the Great to restore the balance. On the other hand, where a work ends fortissimo with the thick chords low down, as in Rheinberger's Sonata No. 7, in F minor, these may sometimes be played with thrilling effect on the Tuba plus octave coupler only, instead of on the full Great as is usually done. In both these somewhat daring experiments, not only must the Tuba be a first-class reed, highly finished, but also be appropriate in tone quality. It is a severe test, but the effect is well worth trying. Its most effective use, however, is in chords by itself against the full flue-work Great to Mixture. This was one of the most striking features of Best's playing at St. George's Hall, Liverpool. Those who care to examine his original compositions and his wonderful arrangements will find admirable examples. The late Mr. H. Heathcote Statham carried this principle further in his registration article in the original edition of Grove, which was surely most advanced for its day. In his excellent book entitled " The Organ and its Position in Musical Art " (1909), he cites passages from J. S. Bach and Mendelssohn showing how this principle may be effectively applied. He concludes with a warning : " This is a power to be used with reserve and caution, and the more reticent is the player in the use of such effects, the greater their impression when introduced : they should never be allowed to degenerate into a commonplace." The last remark is even more true of the coupled Tuba.

Octave and suboctave couplers should be sparingly used, especially the latter. They are best reserved for Strings and fancy effects. In big combinations the suboctave, on its own manual, should be shunned like a plague. Sir Walter Alcock, in his valuable book, " The Organ," gives very sound advice on the subject. It should never be forgotten that, when both are in use, the playing compass is reduced by two octaves, one at each end of the keyboard. Where no Clarion exists on the Swell, the octave coupler may occasionally be used in the full, but to add both to an otherwise complete and well-balanced full Swell is to ruin the effect. An octave coupler is a valuable adjunct to the Solo Organ. No self-respecting organ player abuses the Tremulant. While its too frequent and prolonged use is very irritating to the sensitive listener, its occasional employment for short periods can be quite effective. It is recorded that no less a person than J. S. Bach gave directions for it to be put in order. Evidently he was not above making use of it at times. Many Tremulants beat too quickly.

Some of the general principles which have been explained are peculiarly applicable to the intelligent rendering of Bach, as his organ compositions are largely contrapuntal. It has been said that our modern instruments are unsuitable for interpreting these, and there is some truth in this as they are usually played. On the other hand, if a good modern organ had been then available, Bach would probably have made full use of it in his own particular way, as he was fond of trying experiments. If the player really desires to present this master's wonderful compositions so that they may be intelligible to the ordinary musical listener, conventional registration and treatment must be avoided. To this end, especially if the building be resonant, the playing should be deliberate, the phrasing crisp (even somewhat exaggerated) and the combinations used transparent. Like many modern pianists, some of our foremost players seem to vie with each other as to who can get through a big Bach work in the shortest possible time. His organ compositions were never intended to be treated as mere virtuoso pieces to show off the skill of the player. The Toccata in F, for instance, loses all its dignity if taken at express speed. An excessively quick tempo spreads confusion, and very much increases the listener's difficulty of comprehension. The great Continental players do not make that mistake : they usually play Bach quite deliberately. Uncoupled manuals, with a minimum of 8-ft. and 16-ft. stops, but with bright upperwork, should be employed. Episodal passages are generally more distinct when played on the Swell flue-work with the box open rather than on the Choir, which, in this country, is too feeble, more especially as it is usually enclosed. Clear, but not too heavy, Pedal registers should be used. If the Swell has a good 16-ft. reed it may well be coupled to the Pedal with the box open and the chorus reeds added to it if required. Where there are extensive Pedal passages, as in the great G minor Fugue, relief can sometimes be afforded by playing one or two of them in 8-ft. pitch, if a sufficiently telling Octave Wood is available. Manual chorus reeds are best avoided altogether, especially in rapid contrapuntal passages, as they only spread confusion. The discreet use of the Pedal reed, and, still more rarely, of a manual Solo reed, for some special effect, or to emphasise the entry of a subject which might otherwise be missed, may be permissible, and is a great assistance to the listener. Full Pedal with reeds against full Great to Mixtures without reeds, is a particularly majestic effect, and is historically correct. There are, however, some instruments where, through the Great Organ upperwork being too soft, or the Pedal reed too heavy, this arrangement does not work satisfactorily. Indeed, generalisations about registration must always be tried out with regard to the idiosyncracies of any particular organ. Players on strange instruments should never rely upon the blind application of any rule of thumb, but should exercise their ingenuity to discover the most satisfactory effects, *in the building itself*.

Swell boxes should not be closed. Bach sometimes had one or two manual couplers, but he had no Swell boxes or stop-moving mechanism. His music, being largely of a statuesque character, is independent of Swell crescendos. An example of how not to do it can now be given. One edition directs the use of full Swell for the second section of the great five-voice Fugue in E flat, and it is generally so played. The editor (no less a person than W. T. Best) presumably desired to indicate a contrast with the grave Diapason opening. By the listener at a distance, nothing can be distinguished but a confused, reedy jumble. In the revised edition, Dr. Eaglefield adds: "Box closed"! If this section be played on a good unenclosed Choir, with plenty of upper-work, or, failing that, on some Swell flue-work, with or without the Mixture (the box being fully open) the contrast will be equally marked and the beautiful part-writing clear. In the final climax of the fugue, the Solo reed may well be coupled to the full Pedal, but if the Solo-to-Great be drawn this thrilling entry will be nullified. Much more might be said on this subject, but there should be little difficulty in applying the general principles which have been indicated.

The registration of French organ music in modern times has been almost entirely conditioned by the Cavaillé-Coll organ and its ventil system, which has already been described in Chapter I. For such an instrument were written the great works, in quasi-symphonic style, of Guilmant, César Franck, Widor, the more modern Vierne, Dupré, and others. It is, therefore, a force very much to be reckoned with, but little comment is called for, since copious directions are invariably given in the organ copies. The difficulty is to interpret these effectively on the modern English organ, which has no ventils but is, as a rule, well supplied with stop-moving mechanism, and sometimes with adjustable combinations. It is important to remember that Cavaillé-Coll's flue-work was much lighter and more transparent than ours often is. Consequently, such a direction as " Fonds 8-ft." does not imply a combination of keen Strings, big Flutes and heavy Diapasons, but only an effect such as would be obtained by playing on a small Diapason, or a Geigen with a Stopped Diapason or Harmonic Flute. Again, the Basson-Hautbois is a good deal more piquant than our Swell Oboe ; in fact, it is more like an Orchestral Hautboy or even a small Trumpet. The Cavaillé-Coll organ had no pistons or combination pedals to change the stops, but it had a system of ventils. Each department was provided with two soundboards, one for all the flue-work up to 2-ft., while on the other were Mixtures and chorus reeds. The wind might be excluded from each of these sound-boards by a pedal operating a ventil. The couplers were also pedal-controlled. When playing a piece working up to a full organ, all the stops would be drawn beforehand, but they would be prevented from sounding by the ventils being closed. The manual couplers would also be brought on. The ventils would then be released in turn until the full organ was sounding. On a big five-manual like Nôtre Dame, Paris, where each manual is complete with Mixture and chorus reeds, a very fine build-up and climax can thus be obtained without touching a stop or Swell pedal, or lifting the hands from the Grande Orgue Clavier. On the English organ, however, where effective compound stops and chorus reeds are generally found on the Great and Swell only, the direction "Tous les Claviers acouplis" must be resolutely ignored. It is quite foreign to our methods, and wholly inapplicable to our instruments. So much for the manuals. On the English Pedal it is often difficult to provide an equivalent for the French "Anches Pédales" obligato, in which 8-ft. and 4-ft. reeds play as important a part as the 16-ft. register. As our 16-ft. reeds are weightier, the addition of those in 8-ft. and 4-ft. pitch is even more necessary, in order to do justice to the composer's intentions. The latter registers (especially the 4-ft.) are generally absent from the Pedal, so recourse must be had to coupling the heavy Solo reed in unison and octave pitches. Where the Great reeds are transferable to another manual they may be utilised in the same way.

The registration of early French music has already been dealt with in Chapter II so no further remarks are necessary. In the same chapter it was explained that seventeenth and eighteenth-century registration relied almost exclusively upon the combination of stops of different pitches. The present chapter has already emphasised this in relation to the modern organ, if it is to be displayed to the best effect from the listener's point of view.

This method is even more applicable to the extension organ, on which selective discrimination is most important if unbalanced effects are to be avoided. Let us examine an imaginary three-rank Diapason chorus which may be made up as follows :—

(1) The large open 8-ft. is unextended   ...   61 pipes
(2) A medium-powered rank supplies 8-ft. and 4-ft. stops   73   ,,
(3) A softer rank provides 16-ft., 8-ft., 5⅓-ft., 4-ft., 2⅔-ft. or 2-ft. stops...   97   ,,

A Mixture also may be variously derived. If all the extensions are sounding at once, an unbalanced, " top-and-bottom " effect will result. In full to Fifteenth, for example, it will be more artistic to draw only : The large 8-ft., the 4-ft. stop of the medium-powered rank ; and the 16, 5⅓, 2⅔ and 2-ft. of the softer rank. Thus the effect, for all intents and purposes, will be that of an ordinary chorus. In varied build-up and special effects, however, the wider choice of registers affords a degree of flexibility which could not other-wise be obtained without great expense. We will now give an imaginary example of a three-rank Choir Organ com-prising :—

(1) A small Diapason unit providing 8-ft., 4-ft. and 2-ft. stops...   ...   .   85 pipes
(2) A Lieblich Gedeckt unit providing 16-ft., 4-ft., 8-ft., 2⅔-ft. and 2-ft. stops   ...   97   ,,
(3) A Salicional unit providing 16-ft., 8-ft., 4-ft., 2-ft., 1⅓-ft. and 1-ft. stops   97   ,,

The top octave of the 19th and 22nd break back. For special purposes the whole of any unit could be drawn together, and the result would be quite agreeable. If a combination of quasi-Flute and Diapason tone be desired, more subtle and varied effects are to be obtained by intermingling the units in such a way that the fact of their being extended will hardly be apparent, even to the most acute listener. Here are a few examples :—

(1)
  Diapason 4-ft.
  Salicional 8-ft. and 1⅓-ft.
  Gedeckt 2⅔-ft. and 2-ft.

(2)
  Salicional 16-ft., 4-ft. and 1-ft.
  Gedeckt 8-ft. and 2-ft.

(3)
  Diapason 8-ft. and 2-ft.
  Salicional 4-ft., 1⅓-ft. and 1-ft.
  Gedeckt 16-ft. and 4-ft.

(4)
  Diapason 8-ft. and 4-ft.
  Salicional 2-ft. and 1-ft.
  Gedeckt 16-ft. and 8-ft.

There are a variety of others, but enough has been said to show that while an extension organ may, perhaps, be tolerable if the stops are used promiscuously, it will yield an immense range of subtleties if registered with artistic discrimination.   The science of registration on the extension instrument is almost a new one and so far is clearly understood only by a small minority of our leading players.

In conclusion something must be said concerning the St. Bees Priory organ, which has been referred to more than once, and about its organist Mr. W. M. Coulthard, who did so much experimental work there and elsewhere. The results he obtained have been fully described in this book, which is dedicated to him. This remarkable instrument was built by Henry Willis in 1899, about eighteen months before his death, and was the last important organ to be finished by him personally. It was designed by Mr. F. J. Livesey, who was organist from 1887 till his death in 1934. Though quite moderate in size, it is capable of producing most of the effects one looks for but does not always find in large instruments. The specification is as follows :—

St. Bees Priory Church, Cumberland
(*Henry Willis*, 1899)

Three Manuals CC to A, 58 *notes.*   *Pedals CCC to F*, 30 *notes*

36 *Speaking Stops*   15 *Couplers, etc.*

Pedal Organ

	ft.
Double Open Bass (to G, 21⅓-ft. (18 from Open Bass)	32
Sub-Bass Stopped Wood	16
Open Diapason (from Great) ... ... Metal	16
Open Bass ... Wood	16
Flute (18 from Sub-Bass) Wood	8
Octave (18 from Open Bass) ... ... Wood	8
Ophicleide ... Metal	16
Double Ophicleide (18 from Ophicleide) ...	32

Solo to Pedal
Great to Pedal
Swell to Pedal
Six Combination Pedals
Three Pistons to Pedal
Couplers

Solo Organ (lower Manual)
Enclosed

		ft.
Double Salicional (12 Wood) ... ... Metal		16
Viol D'Amour ... ,,		8
Voix Célestes (Ten. C) ,,		8
Claribel Flute (Stopped Bass) ... ... Wood		8
Concert Flute ... Metal		4
Harmonic Piccolo ... ,,		2
Orchestral Clarinet ,,		8

Tremulant
Lever Swell Pedal

Unenclosed

Tuba Mirabilis (Harmonic) Metal 8

Octave
Swell to Solo
Five Pistons

GREAT ORGAN

	ft.
Double Open Diapason Metal	16
Stopped Diapason Wood	8
Hohl Flöte (open through-out) ... ... Wood	8
Open Diapason ... Metal	8
Wald Flöte (open through-out) ... ... Wood	4
Principal ... ... Metal	4
Twelfth ... ... ,,	2⅔
Fifteenth ... ... ,,	2
Cornet, 17, 19, 22 ... ,,	III
Tromba (harmonic trebles)	8
Clarion (harmonic trebles)	4

Solo Suboctave to Great
Solo to Great
Swell to Great
Great Pistons to Combination
  Pedals
Five Pistons
Reversible Pedal to Solo to
  Great
Reversible Pedal to Swell to
  Great

SWELL ORGAN

		ft.
Open Diapason ... Metal		8
Gemshorn ... ... ,,		4
Flageolet ... ... ,,		2
Mixture 12, 19, 22 ... ,,		III
Vox Humana ... ,,		8

Tremulant

Oboe	8
Contra Posaune	16
Cornopean	8
Clarion	4

Lever Swell Pedal
Five Pistons (one for Pedal
  Solo)

COMBINATION COUPLERS

Pedal and Accomp. to Solo
  Pistons
Pedal to Great Pistons
Pedal to Swell Pistons
Swell Pistons to Combination
  Pedals

WIND PRESSURES :

Pedal flue-work : 3, 3½ and 4½ inches ; Reed : 15 and 16 inches.
Manual flue-work with Clarinet and Vox Humana : 3½ inches.
Chorus reeds and Oboe : 7 inches. Tuba : 15 inches.
Action wind : 12 and 16 inches.

The action is tubular pneumatic. All the combinations are
  easily adjustable by switchboard.

There are four spare slides.

Mr. Coulthard is Cumbrian bred and born. He is a school-master by profession,* with music as a side line. He was one of Dr. F. W. Wadely's most gifted and distinguished pupils, to whose efficient training he owes much. He is an exceptionally fine Bach exponent. After he came to St. Bees, in 1936, he was naturally inspired by the splendour of the Willis organ, and developed a style of playing and registration all his own. As the combination settings at which he arrived, after numerous experiments, are so interesting, and illustrate much of what has been said in this chapter, they are here given :—

Mr. Coulthard's Combination Settings

Pedal Combination Pedals

1. (Pedal solo) Open Wood 32-ft. and 8-ft.; Reed 16-ft.
2. Sub-Bass 16-ft. Flute 8-ft.
3. Open Wood 16-ft.
4. Open Wood 32-ft. Open Metal 16-ft.
5. Open Wood 32-ft. and 16-ft.
6. (Full Pedal) Open Wood 32-ft., 16-ft. and 8-ft. Reed 16-ft. and 32-ft.

Choir Solo Organ Pistons

1. Salicional 16-ft. Flutes 8-ft., 4-ft. and 2-ft.
2. Flutes 8-ft. and 4-ft.
3. Clarinet 8-ft.
4. Salicional 16-ft., Viole 8-ft., and Octave Coupler.
5. Tuba.

Great Organ Pistons

1. Stopped Diapason 8-ft. and Wald Flöte 4-ft.
2. Open Diapason 8-ft. and Principal 4-ft.
3. Diapasons 16-ft., 8-ft., 4-ft., 2⅔-ft. and 2-ft.
4. Diapasons 16-ft., 8-ft., 4-ft., 2⅔-ft., 2-ft. and III.
5. Full Great—Diapasons 16-ft., 8-ft., 2⅔-ft., 2-ft. and III, Reeds 8-ft. and 4-ft., withdraws Swell to Great.

---

* During the war he served for five-and-a-half years in the Royal Artillery, and rose to the rank of Captain.

Swell Organ Pistons

1. Diapasons 8-ft. and 4-ft.
2. Diapasons 8-ft., 4-ft., 2-ft. and III.
3. Cornopean 8-ft.
4. Full Swell—diapasons 2-ft. and III, Reeds 16-ft., 8-ft. and 4-ft.
5. Pedal Solo—Contra Posaune 16-ft. and Swell to Pedal.

All speaking stops not named are taken in. It should be noted that the Principal 4-ft. and the Swell-to-Great coupler are withdrawn from the Full Great, and the Hohl-Flöte and Swell Oboe do not enter into any set combination. The manual flue-work and reeds are kept entirely separate, except on the Full Great and Full Swell pistons. The other tone families, also, are not mixed so that plenty of contrast is secured. Not more than one 16-ft. stop on the Pedal and one 8-ft. on the manuals are drawn except in the full. The method of combining registers of *different* pitches has, however, been fully exploited. To be at the console with Mr. Coulthard is to receive an object lesson in unconventional combinations and economy of registration. Of the thirty-six speaking stops at present available, each one will probably be heard at some time or other but never more than about a dozen will be sounding at once. The Swell-to-Great is drawn only when required, and, though climaxes are well marked, the Tuba is but rarely coupled. At a distance the registration sounds clear, effective and telling. Such economy in the use of stops produces results vastly different from the colourless muddle of sound apparently beloved by most players, which has brought the King of Instruments into not unreasonable disrepute among the ordinary musical public.

Bibliography

"THE ORGAN," a Quarterly Review published by Musical Opinion Ltd.

THE ENCYCLOPAEDIA BRITANNICA.

A STUDENT'S GUIDE TO THE ORGAN, by R. Whitworth, M.B.E.

THE ELECTRIC ORGAN, by R. Whitworth, M.B.E.

THE MODERN BRITISH ORGAN, by the Rev. N. A. Bonavia Hunt.

J. S. BACH, a Biography by C. Sanford Terry.

J. S. BACH, by Dr. A. Schweitzer (translated by E. Newman).

L'ESTHETIQUE DE L'ORGUE, by Jean Huré.

Index